Adding the Lone Star

LANDMARK PRESIDENTIAL DECISIONS

Series Editor
Michael Nelson

Advisory Board
Meena Bose
Brendan J. Doherty
Richard J. Ellis
Lori Cox Han
James Oakes
Barbara A. Perry
Andrew Rudalevige

Adding the Lone Star

John Tyler, Sam Houston, and the Annexation of Texas

Jordan T. Cash

© 2024 by the University Press of Kansas
All rights reserved

Published by the University Press of Kansas (Lawrence, Kansas 66045), which was organized by the Kansas Board of Regents and is operated and funded by Emporia State University, Fort Hays State University, Kansas State University, Pittsburg State University, the University of Kansas, and Wichita State University.

Library of Congress Cataloging-in-Publication Data

Names: Cash, Jordan T., author.
Title: Adding the lone star : John Tyler, Sam Houston, and the annexation of Texas / Jordan T. Cash.
Other titles: John Tyler, Sam Houston, and the annexation of Texas
Description: Lawrence, Kansas : University Press of Kansas, 2024. | Series: Landmark presidential decisions | Includes bibliographical references and index.
Identifiers: LCCN 2023029007 (print) | LCCN 2023029008 (ebook)
  ISBN 9780700636389 (cloth)
  ISBN 9780700636365 (paperback)
  ISBN 9780700636372 (ebook)
Subjects: LCSH: Texas—Annexation to the United States. | Texas—History—To 1846. | United States—Politics and government—1841–1845. | Tyler, John, 1790–1862. | Houston, Sam, 1793–1863.
Classification: LCC F390 .C367 2024 (print) | LCC F390 (ebook) | DDC 976.4/04—dc23/eng/20230907
LC record available at https://lccn.loc.gov/2023029007.
LC ebook record available at https://lccn.loc.gov/2023029008.

British Library Cataloguing-in-Publication Data is available.

Printed in the United States of America

10 9 8 7 6 5 4 3 2 1

The paper used in this publication is acid free and meets the minimum requirements of the American National Standard for Permanence of Paper for Printed Library Materials Z39.48-1992.

*To Catherine and Alexander.
Your father loves you very much.*

CONTENTS

Foreword   ix

Acknowledgments   xi

Introduction: Not One, but Two Presidents   1

Chapter 1. The Tex-Mex Executive   6

Chapter 2. His Accidency, John Tyler   16

Chapter 3. Sam Houston and the Republic of Texas   31

Chapter 4. The Annexation Treaty   48

Chapter 5. The Elections of 1844   70

Conclusion: The Primacy of Presidential Policymaking   93

Notes   109

Bibliographic Essay   135

Index   145

FOREWORD

There is a clear bias among those who study the American presidency to focus primarily on the post-1932 world. In this reading of history Franklin Roosevelt fundamentally changed the office—changed it so fundamentally that the presidency after 1932 is really a different type of institution than before. Therefore, there is little use in studying the "premodern" presidency, other than as a historical oddity. Thus, 144 years of presidential history and data are consigned to irrelevancy.

The problem with this perspective is that there are a host of phenomena connected to the modern presidency that are present in its premodern manifestations—so many, in fact, that it begs the question whether it makes sense to bifurcate the office at 1932. To list just a few: the constitutional structure of the presidency (composed of one individual), the power problem created by a separation of powers system, the formal and implied powers of the office, the party structure of which it is an essential part, the connection between "mandates" and election results, the central concern over the security and stability of the nation, the character qualities (political skill, managerial talent, policy vision) of the individual inhabiting the office—each of these items is the focus of significant scholarship, and all of them are key features of presidents going all the way back to George Washington.

If one wanted to look for a test case of this argument—a premodern president who appears to be the precise opposite of Franklin Roosevelt—one could hardly do better than John Tyler. He was an accidental president whose legitimacy was questioned by many of his peers. Unelected, partyless (in large part by his own actions), facing fierce opposition in Congress, no claim to a mandate, as close to a lame duck as one could get for most of his term, facing a foreign policy conundrum that could easily lead to war with Mexico, and which also invited the interest of presumably stronger European powers, all while agitating and energizing the most divisive and controversial domestic policy issue—slavery. That was the issue Tyler faced in the early 1840s with the annexation of the Republic of Texas.

In this volume Jordan Cash performs two singular services. First, in exploring Tyler's role in the Texas annexation effort, Cash demonstrates the enduring benefits of studying presidents from across all of American history. The challenges Tyler faced—partisan, electoral, administrative, domestic, international security—are connected tightly to the structural features of the constitutional position, and the powers (written and unwritten) of the office wielded by the individual. And those are timeless features of this institution. Second, by expanding his analysis to include Sam Houston of the Republic of Texas, Cash performs a comparative analysis of two different "American" presidents, operating under two different but related constitutional systems, facing different political, institutional, and foreign policy challenges. Two presidents, in two different political contexts, facing the same basic issue.

Jordan Cash highlights enduring features of the Anglo-American constitutional tradition, and the nature and practice of executive power within that tradition, that resonate down to the present. Readers of this book will learn about an important policy effort in American history, but they will also be reminded of the challenges and opportunities of executive leadership—challenges and opportunities that have remained remarkably constant from Washington through Biden. This book is a significant contribution to our knowledge and understanding of executive power.

David A. Crockett

ACKNOWLEDGMENTS

In writing this book I have been fortunate to have received help and encouragement from many different people. Curt Nichols first made me aware of the new series on Landmark Presidential Decisions at the University Press of Kansas and encouraged me to propose a book on John Tyler and Texas annexation in the first place. Series editor Michael Nelson was enthusiastic about my idea of comparing the American and Texian presidencies and has remained unwavering in his support of the project. I benefitted greatly from the insights shared by David Clinton and am thankful for his help in pointing me to a wealth of information that was crucial in understanding the intricacies of nineteenth-century diplomacy. I am also extremely grateful for the invaluable work of my research assistant Joseph Natali. It is no exaggeration to say that this book is much better because of his efforts, and I look forward to seeing all the amazing work he does in the future. The Texas Collection at Baylor University was a wonderful resource in finding materials on the early history of Texas, and it was fortuitous that I was at Baylor during the early stages of this project. At the University Press of Kansas, David Congdon has been a pleasure to work with, and I am very thankful for his patience and direction, as well as for the helpful suggestions of the two anonymous reviewers. I am also thankful for the support and encouragement of my colleagues in James Madison College at Michigan State University. Most of all, I am grateful to my family for their constant love and support. My wife Kim has supported me throughout this entire process and indulged my interest in the history of the Republic of Texas. My daughter Catherine, who was born in Texas while I was writing this book, and my son Alexander, who was born while this book was in production, have been unceasing sources of love and joy, and it is to them that this book is dedicated.

INTRODUCTION

Not One, but Two Presidents

Since the founding of the United States in 1776, thirty-seven states have been added to the original thirteen. While the admission of a new state is always of immense political importance, no single state's entry into the Union had as great an impact as that of Texas.

In foreign policy, the annexation of a state which Mexico claimed was still a part of its union put the United States onto a collision course with its southern neighbor. The resulting Mexican War killed thousands and saw the United States acquire what is now California, Nevada, Utah, and parts of Arizona, New Mexico, Colorado, and Wyoming. Domestically, the addition of Texas exemplified Americans' commitment to westward expansion, and it was during the debate over Texas that the famous phrase "manifest destiny" was coined.[1] Yet even while Texas highlighted the increasing importance of the West, its status as a new slave state unbalanced the political equilibrium between Northern free states and Southern slave states, exacerbating sectional tensions which exploded into civil war—and Texas' own attempted secession—a mere sixteen years later. In short, transforming the Lone Star Republic into the Lone Star State created numerous complications and controversies which significantly contributed to the destabilization of the entire American political system.

These facts have long been noted by scholars who have described the annexation of Texas as a turning point in American history and a critical event in the lead-up to the Civil War. Historian William Freehling considered Texas' incorporation into the Union to be "the largest turning point on the road to disunion."² Similarly, Joel Silbey went so far as to insist that "the conflict over annexation *and*, most particularly, the political fallout from it, has fair claim to be considered as *the* critical base point on which the rest of the crisis of the Union grew."³

Others have highlighted the role of slavery in driving Texas to declare independence from Mexico and to then seek to join the United States. Randolph Campbell notes that while slavery was not the primary cause of the Texas Revolution, it was a contributing factor, and the continuing protection of the peculiar institution was a "major result."⁴ More starkly, Andrew Torget contends that the Texians' pursuit of annexation was an effort to save their vision of a slave-driven agricultural empire.⁵

Contemporaries also commented on the link between Texas and the sectional politics of the time. Frederick Douglass repeatedly cited Texas' admission to the Union as a victory for the "slave power."⁶ Similarly, Ulysses S. Grant insisted in his *Memoirs* that the "the occupation, separation, and annexation" of Texas "were, from the inception of the movement to its final consummation, a conspiracy to acquire territory out of which slave states might be formed for the American Union." While Grant does not connect annexation directly to the Civil War—and admits that Texas itself was "of incalculable value"—he does remark that "the Southern rebellion was largely the outgrowth of the Mexican war," which had only emerged from "taking military possession of Texas after annexation."⁷

Given the importance of Texas' annexation as a national turning point, a full understanding of the antebellum era and the origins of the Civil War is incomplete without taking account of the reasons and methods used to add Texas to the Union. Yet to comprehend those reasons and methods, we must focus primarily on the actions of the man most responsible for annexation: President John Tyler.

Annexing Texas was the most significant accomplishment of Tyler's administration, and it is a central event in all major biographies of Tyler.⁸ Indeed, studies of Tyler have frequently cited his actions during annexation as an example of robust unilateral presidential power, with David Crockett noting that Tyler's annexation triumph was "based largely on his use of prerogative powers."⁹ A growing body of research further suggests that even while Tyler was not the most successful or popular president, he used his executive authority effectively.[10] Robert Spitzer provides the most succinct description of Tyler's paradoxical presidency in remarking that that despite Tyler's "weak and failed presidency," his administration "proved to be one of the most important in framing, resolving, and advancing constitutionally based executive power."[11]

Yet Tyler was not the only American serving as a national executive during the debates over annexation; he had a counterpart in Sam Houston, the concurrently serving president of the Republic of Texas. These two presidents, born roughly 150 miles apart in Virginia—the "Mother of Presidents"—together accomplished one of the most important territorial expansions in American history and irrevocably shifted the antebellum political landscape. Their simultaneous handling of annexation provides students and scholars of executive power with the unique opportunity to examine two American-style presidents serving at the same time, working on the same issue, but from two radically different institutional and political situations. While there is a growing literature on comparative presidentialism in Latin American countries,[12] the lack of presidential systems in Anglophone countries has largely prevented a direct comparison of the presidencies which emerged out of the Anglo-American legal and political tradition.

This book's dual examination of Tyler and Houston fills that gap while also enabling us to better perceive the nuances and conditions which affect how American presidents use their constitutional, institutional, and political authority. Specifically, assessing Tyler and Houston side-by-side grants us three crucial insights into presidential power.

First, we shall see that despite their differing structural, institutional, and political situations, both presidents were constitutionally positioned to direct their nations' respective foreign policies, illustrating the immense influence and control presidents have in foreign affairs. In Tyler's case this is particularly notable, as he was deprived of nearly all the external institutional and political supports that presidents normally rely on. In Houston's case, it is significant because Texas' standing as a small and weak republic meant its survival depended on having a foreign policy that could navigate the competing interests of the United States, Mexico, and major European powers. That Houston was situated to craft that foreign policy points to the importance of the individual wielding presidential power and the agency available to presidents in steering their nations' diplomatic and military agendas.

Second, by including Houston in a discussion of American presidential power, we can observe the ways in which slight variations in American constitutional practice may affect presidential behavior. Moreover, Houston's immense popularity provides further evidence of how popular support can bolster presidential actions and enable presidents to overcome institutional obstacles in a constitutional system of separation of powers.

Finally, considering the different sizes and relative strengths of the two republics, these presidents demonstrate the possibilities available for American-style executives in responding to diverse geopolitical conditions. Texas' status as a small, weak nation without subnational states allows us to evaluate Houston as an example of how an American executive may employ his authority when governing a vulnerable unitary republic. Tyler, by contrast, gives us a view of how presidential power can be wielded by the chief executive of an emerging great power. These differing positions in the international order had a significant effect on the amount of agency these presidents were able to exercise in their decision-making regarding annexation, providing lessons that can be generalized to other presidents and institutional environments.

As the purpose of this book is to utilize the unique comparative opportunity presented by the annexation of Texas to better understand presidential power, my intent is not to present a comprehensive history of annexation. Rather, my focus throughout the book is how the presidents involved in annexation approached the problem and how their differing constitutional, institutional, and political contexts affected their choices and actions in office. In some areas, therefore, I may not touch on particular historical details, emphasizing instead the arguments and actions undertaken by the major political figures directly involved in annexation.

To provide the foundation for comparing the Tyler and Houston administrations over the rest of this book, chapter one assesses the constitutional systems of the United States and Texas, specifically highlighting the executives created by those two systems. Chapter two introduces

John Tyler and discusses his life and presidency up to October 1841, when he began actively considering Texas annexation as a major policy goal. This chapter pays particular attention to Tyler's previous support of expansionist policies and his pre-presidential views on executive power. Chapter three then explores the United States' relationship with Texas, including Texas' role in American foreign policy in the early nineteenth century and attempts at annexation made by the administrations preceding Tyler. This chapter also provides the background for Sam Houston up to his second term as the president of Texas, which began in late December 1841. From there, the narratives converge as chapter four examines the diplomatic maneuverings and negotiations which resulted in an annexation treaty, including the role of slavery, and analyzes the debates which led to the treaty's failure in the US Senate. Chapter five then evaluates how Tyler and Houston dealt with that initial failure, and the role the 1844 presidential elections in both the United States and Texas played in the final push for annexation. It also briefly addresses the aftermath of annexation and the last years of Tyler and Houston. Finally, the conclusion compares the two presidents directly to derive lessons on how the different conditions each man faced affected their use of executive power, as well as touching on how the methods used to accomplish annexation set precedents which later American presidents adopted for their own efforts at territorial expansion.

The American presidency has historically acted as the focal point of American politics. But the paucity of similarly structured presidencies in the Anglo-American constitutional tradition has limited our ability to make clear comparisons with countries that have similar historical and legal contexts. With the Texian presidency, however, we have the rare opportunity to see what happens when there is not just one American president, but two.

CHAPTER 1

The Tex-Mex Executive

In order to compare Tyler's and Houston's actions in office, we must first compare the structures, duties, and powers of the American and Texian presidencies, which itself requires an assessment of the 1836 Constitution of the Republic of Texas.

The Constitution of the Republic of Texas

The convention which drafted the American constitution of 1787 engaged in intense deliberations and carefully constructed what became the governing document of the United States government over course of nearly four months. By contrast, the convention which drafted the Texas constitution of 1836 did so in roughly two weeks at the height of the Texas Revolution. With the Alamo under siege by Mexican forces—it fell while the convention was in session—the Texians' deliberations were harried by "a sense of military urgency" which threatened to break up the convention several times.[1] Nevertheless, between March 1 and March 17, 1836, the delegates managed to write and adopt a declaration of independence, appoint Houston as commander in chief of the ragtag force generously referred to as the "Army of Texas," and draft and adopt a constitution.[2]

A majority of the delegates who drafted the 1836 constitution were American by birth—primarily from the South[3]—and had only been in Texas a short time. As Paul Lack points out, nearly half of the delegates had been in Texas for less than two years, and a substantial number of those had emigrated during the previous year. Some of the most prominent delegates, such as George C. Childress, the author of the Texas Declaration of Independence, had only resided in Texas for a few months before being elected to the convention.[4] A few delegates also had experience in American politics, with a handful even having participated in drafting state constitutions in Alabama (1819), Missouri (1819), and North Carolina (1835), respectively.[5] That so many of the delegates were Americans is notable, as this is one of the very few instances where Americans after 1787 had the opportunity to write a national constitution.[6]

Yet not all the delegates were American. Two, José Antonio Navarro and José Francisco Ruiz, were Tejanos—Texas-born descendants of the original Spanish settlers. Notably, the most experienced delegate at the convention was a Mexican statesman, Lorenzo de Zavala. Zavala had held a wide variety of high-level positions in Mexican politics, including serving as president of the Constituent Congress which drafted the Mexican Constitution of 1824.[7] The convention's mix of Anglo and Latino delegates, as well as the Texas revolutionaries' early insistence that they were fighting to restore the discarded Mexican Constitution of 1824,[8] directs us to consider the influence of Mexican constitutionalism in any discussion of Texian institutions.

On the surface, both the Mexican constitution of 1824 and the Texian constitution of 1836 appear to be derivative of the American constitution, creating a bicameral legislature, single executive, and independent judiciary. Even the French political philosopher and foremost observer of American democracy, Alexis de Tocqueville, asserted that Mexico had "copied almost entirely the federal constitution of the Anglo-Americans, their neighbors."[9] Similarly, most scholars have dismissed the Texas constitution as "var[ying] scarcely at all from its [American] model."[10]

Recent research, however, shows that the Mexicans were far more influenced by their Spanish constitutional heritage than by their neighbors to the north, modeling their constitution on the Spanish constitution of 1812, albeit with significant alterations "adopted to address Mexico's new reality."[11] Similarly, there are subtle but important differences between the Texas constitution and its American antecedent which are discussed later in this chapter. During the debate on annexation, Kentucky senator Henry Clay went so far as to claim that "whilst Texas has adopted our Constitution as the model of hers, she has, in several important particulars, greatly improved upon it."[12]

Texas also had its own constitutional heritage at the state level. It had been governed by the state constitution of Coahuila y Tejas since 1827, and in 1833, a convention of Tejanos and Texians had petitioned Mexico to make Texas into a distinct Mexican state, even proposing a new state constitution. Notably, the committee which drew up the proposed constitution was chaired by none other than Sam Houston.[13]

Considering these influences and prior history, a full evaluation of the constitutional elements of the Texian presidency must compare it not only to the American and Mexican presidencies, but also to the state executives in the 1827 Coahuiltexian constitution and the proposed 1833 constitution. Unfortunately, the official journal of the 1836 Texas convention only recorded procedural motions rather than the substance of the debates, and the main text of the constitution was drafted in a committee whose records are not extant. Thus, we do not know the specific rationale for the various contours of the Texian executive.[14] Nonetheless, by examining the different constitutions and their provisions concerning the executive, we will not only see what the Texians—both Anglo and Latino—chose to change about the American constitutional model when given a chance, but we will also observe whether those changes are a legacy of Mexican constitutional principles or innovations of the Texians themselves. Combining these constitutional variations with the differing institutional and political situations Tyler and Houston faced will enable us to have a more complete understanding of how these varying conditions affected the ways in which Tyler and Houston pursued annexation.

Comparing the Executives

Many of the structural elements and powers held by the American and Texian executives are quite similar. Structurally, they both consist of a single president with a minimum age requirement of thirty-five years old. Each president also possesses a qualified veto that can be overridden by a two-thirds vote of both houses of Congress; a treaty power that requires two-thirds of the Senate to ratify; an appointment power that requires the Senate to advise and consent to nominations, as well as a recess appointment power for when the Senate is out of session; the authority to receive foreign ministers; and a pardon power that can be used in all cases except impeachment. Moreover, the standards for impeaching the presidents upon charges of treason, bribery, or other high crimes and misdemeanors are nearly identical.[15] Yet there are some important differences, several of which may be attributed to the Lone Star Republic's constitutional heritage.

First, the term length for the Texas presidency is shorter, three years as opposed to four, and the first president would have an even shorter term of two years. This term is not only shorter than the American presidency, but also briefer than the Mexican and the Coahuiltexian executives, all of which adopt a four-year term. It is, however, closer to the proposed 1833 Texas constitution and several American state constitutions which set a term of two years for the executive. Nonetheless, no other constitution adopts a different term for the first president, allowing succeeding presidents to have longer terms.[16] Notably, Texian representatives and senators also had shorter terms than their American and Mexican counterparts, with one- and three-year terms, respectively.[17] Given that the terms were shorter across the board, it suggests that the Texians had a preference for short terms akin to that expressed by the Anti-Federalists during the American constitutional ratification debates.[18]

Combined with the provisions on reelection, the shortened terms further indicate an antipathy to executive power. Texas presidents were barred from running for reelection, but they could run for a nonconsecutive term after an intervening three years. This was a major break from American constitutional practice, which at the time had no constitutional limitations on presidents running for reelection.[19] But it was consistent with the Mexican and Coahuiltexian constitutions, both of which had similar provisions forcing presidents to step down after a single term while allowing for reelection after a period of time.[20] In the proposed 1833 constitution, governors could not serve more than four years out of every six, providing more flexibility to those who might seek to run for a second consecutive term, but still insisting on a period of ineligibility.[21]

Several other aspects of the Texian president's powers were more circumscribed than his American counterpart in ways that resembled the Mexican and Coahuiltexian executives. We see this particularly with the Texas presidency's military powers. The American president is made "Commander in Chief of the Army and Navy" and of "the Militia of the several States."[22] The restrictions on the American executive's military power emerge from the fact that significant military authority is vested in Congress, particularly the power to declare war, raise troops, call out the militia, appropriate funds, and provide rules for military administration.[23] Yet once put into service, the American president is virtually unrestricted in how he leads the military during wartime, and he may even lead troops in person, as George Washington did during the Whiskey Rebellion.[24] The constitutions of Mexico, Coahuila y Tejas, and Texas also gave authority over organizing the military—or the militia in the case of Coahuila y Tejas—to the legislature while making the executive commander in chief, but they restrained how and when the executive could command troops. Specifically, the executives in the Mexican, Coahuiltexian, Texian, and proposed 1833 constitutions were all prohibited from personally leading the military unless authorized by the legislature. In the case of Mexico and Coahuila y Tejas, if the executives took the field they would have to surrender their non-military duties to the vice president or vice governor, respectively.[25] By contrast, the Texian vice president would only exercise the powers and duties of the president in the event of the latter's impeachment, removal, death, resignation, or absence, instances which are broader than those allowed under the American constitution, but also slightly more limited than those allowed under the Mexican and Coahuiltexian constitutions.[26]

Interestingly, during the American ratification debates, some Anti-Federalists argued that the president should not be able to personally command troops without the consent of Congress.[27] Such a complaint speaks to the concerns early Americans had about the dangers of an executive possessing strong military authority. Although the Americans did not constitutionalize those concerns, Mexico did. It is, therefore, significant that Texas threaded the needle between these two traditions, following Mexico in not allowing the executive to command in person without legislative sanction, but also following the Americans in not forcing the president to delegate his regular authority to the vice president in the event that he does assume personal command.

The Texian president's appointment power is also somewhat constrained in a manner that reflects the Mexican constitutional heritage. Of the five executives, only the American has the power to appoint members of both the executive and judicial branches. In the proposed 1833 constitution, judges were to be elected independently of either the governor or the legislature. In the other three, judges were appointed by the legislature.[28] Legislative appointment of judges was also common in American state constitutions, including those which some of the Texas delegates had helped draft.[29] Thus, we may see the decision not to allow the Texas president to appoint members of the judiciary as simultaneously an expression of previous Mexican practice and reflective of the influence of the Texas delegates' home state traditions. In either case, it is a restriction that does not exist within the American national constitution and effectively eliminates any influence the Texas president might have over the judicial branch, narrowing his authority more strictly to the executive branch.[30]

In selecting the executive, however, Texas broke from both the American and Mexican models. The former utilized an Electoral College to select the president, while the latter had state legislatures elect the president.[31] Texas instead embraced popular election for the president, vice president, and the Senate.[32] Given that Coahuila y Tejas and the proposed 1833 constitution also had popular election for the governor,[33] one could reasonably argue that the Texians were simply continuing what they already knew. This election model could also be attributed to the lack of a federalist structure. The American and Mexican presidential selection processes both heavily rely on the states in electing the president. Texas, as a unitary republic, lacked those subnational units and could not easily recreate those systems, highlighting the role of circumstance in constitutional construction. Yet the decision to retain popular election was not inevitable. Just as they created new districts for the Texas Senate, districts could have been created to act as a kind of Electoral College. Moreover, legislative selection—which was still utilized in several American states[34]—could have been used for the presidency.

If we place the Texians within the broader context of American political development, we may surmise why they opted for popular election of the executive. Electoral College reform was a major issue in the United States before and after the Texas Revolution. Indeed, it had already been reformed once with the ratification of the Twelfth Amendment in 1804, specifying that electors must cast separate votes for president and vice president, a change whose language is reflected in the Texas constitution which also distinguishes between the selection of those two offices.[35] In the 1820s and 1830s, those efforts escalated, with American president Andrew Jackson even arguing in his first annual message to Congress that the American constitution should be amended "to remove all intermediate agency in the election of the President and Vice President."[36] The goal of many of these reform efforts was to make the presidential selection system more democratic and representative.[37] The Texians' choice of popular election suggests they observed the alternatives—Electoral College and legislative selection—heard the debates of the time, and chose to retain the Coahuiltexian arrangement that had operated during their time as a state.

While the foregoing differences all appear to be connected at least partially to Texas' history as a part of Mexico, drawing either directly from the Mexican constitution or from the state-level constitutions that preceded the revolution, there are other features of the Texas presidency that are unique to it. The most notable is the president's removal power. The American constitution famously does not specify whether or not the president has the power to unilaterally remove his subordinates within the executive branch. The lack of an explicit provision on the subject spurred a debate among the American founders which still continues in Supreme Court jurisprudence.[38] In *Federalist 77*, Alexander Hamilton argued that the president would need the Senate's consent "to displace as well as to appoint,"[39] while in the First Congress James Madison contended that the president possessed unilateral removal authority to ensure that executive subordinates were responsible to him, and by extension, to the people.[40]

Madison's arguments won out in 1789, but the debate reignited only a few years before the Texas constitution was drafted. Jackson became notorious for his aggressive use of the removal power, and he was vigorously opposed by members of the Whig Party who claimed that Jackson was engaged in "executive usurpation."[41] The Whigs' leader, and Jackson's main foe in Congress, the aforementioned Henry Clay, even introduced several resolutions arguing for the Senate to be involved in removals.[42] While Clay's resolutions did not succeed, his efforts are indicative of the fact that the removal debate was a live issue in the 1830s and one which many of the American settlers in Texas would have been aware of.

Alternatively, the Mexican constitution was explicit in giving the president a removal power, enabling him "to appoint and remove at pleasure secretaries of state."[43] The constitution of Coahuila y Tejas also empowered the governor to "freely appoint and remove the secretary of state."[44] Yet even with this explicit removal power, Mexican presidents did not have free rein over their administrations. The Mexican constitution included a council of government "composed of half the senate, one from each state" which was given specific duties independent of the president. Moreover, Mexican cabinet members possessed particular duties to report to the legislature, creating what Jaime Rodriguez Ordóñez called a "quasi-parliamentary system" favoring "congressional superiority."[45] The Coahuiltexian executive had a similar structure and disbursement of powers.[46] The proposed constitution of 1833 followed the American in not addressing the removal power, but it followed the Mexican in not allowing for a unitary executive branch, having the state treasurer be independently elected by the legislature, an idea which had been rejected by the American founders but featured in many state constitutions.[47]

Compared to these models, the Texian executive clearly differentiates itself. Like the American executive—but unlike the Mexican or Coahuiltexian—it does not have a council, nor does it specify the responsibilities of the cabinet members. Aside from stating that the president shall appoint a secretary of state, all other cabinet positions are left to be created by Congress.[48] Yet unlike all the other executives, the Texian constitution specifies that the president can only remove subordinates "with the advice and consent of the Senate."[49] In doing so, the Texians rejected the Mexican approach to the removal power while still choosing to constitutionalize a power the American constitution was silent on, thereby avoiding the contentious disputes that the American founders had endured and which their contemporaries in the United States were continuing to wrestle with. The fact that the removal power was not mentioned in the proposed 1833 constitution also highlights how the Texians were paying attention to debates in the United States. The proposed Texas state constitution was written in April 1833, but the primary controversy over Jackson's removals did not occur until September 1833. Moreover, Clay's resolutions limiting the removal power were not introduced until March 1834. Thus, the authors of the proposed 1833 constitution likely would not have felt a need to clarify the removal power, as it was not a major controversy when it was drafted. But by 1836, the delegates who wrote the constitution would have been keenly aware of such a major constitutional dispute only a few years earlier. This slight change is another indication of how the Texians were attentive to the contemporaneous political debates taking place in the United States.

Beyond merely responding to developments on the American political scene, the Texians' choice to constitutionalize senatorial consent is also significant. The de facto position of the United States at the time—and largely ever since—was unilateral presidential removal. In choosing senatorial consent, the Texians chose the position that prominent American founders in the First Congress had decided against, and which pushed back against the predominant view of the Jacksonian era. Most importantly for this analysis, the Texians' embrace of senatorial consent weakened the presidency. The president would not be able to remove his subordinates at will, but executive officers would be partially responsible to the Senate which had confirmed their appointment and could block their removal. Thus, not only is this an example of the Texians distinguishing their constitution from both the American and Mexican traditions but doing so at the expense of executive power.

When we consider all these provisions from the five constitutions together, we can see that even while the Texian constitution most resembles its American counterpart, the Texians were clearly influenced by their Mexican constitutional heritage. Most of that influence, however, redounded to the diminishment of executive power. Given the weakness of the Mexican constitutional presidency, such a result is not surprising. Whenever the Texians drew from the Mexican—and more broadly Hispanic—constitutional tradition, it was likely going to be to the detriment of the presidency. The elements which we might consider as empowering the Texian presidency are those which are modeled on the American executive.

Yet even the changes they made which drew from American politics, such as the popularly elected president and senatorial consent for removal, came from different aspects of the American political tradition. Looked at from the American perspective, the Texas constitution mixed the contemporary and competing perspectives of the Jacksonian Democrats and the Whigs. In short, when given the opportunity to write a new national constitution and construct a new presidency, the Texians chose to integrate elements that limited executive power. Part of the reason for that decision may be contextual. Their revolution was largely a reaction to Mexican president Santa Anna's strong use of executive power in establishing a dictatorship over Mexico. With such a background it is not surprising that the Texians were wary of executive power in a manner that is similar to that expressed by Americans after the American Revolution.[50] But even apart from that context, when the Texians looked at these various traditions, they picked and chose whatever best suited them, forming an amalgamation of antebellum American constitutional thought and early Mexican constitutionalism.

From this analysis, we can see that despite the immense similarities between the American and Texian presidencies, the latter has more constitutional limitations than the former. In assessing Tyler and Houston, therefore, we can begin with the assumption that the constitutional baseline of power provided to Houston is slightly lower than that provided to Tyler. Knowing where each president is starting from in terms of their constitutional authority will enable us to observe whether the slight variations in power affected Tyler and Houston's actions relative to each other. Furthermore, it will allow us to better understand how other institutional and political factors played into their ability to direct annexation policy.

CHAPTER 2

His Accidency, John Tyler

Born on March 29, 1790, John Tyler was raised in the upper echelons of the Virginia aristocracy. He could trace his lineage back to Virginia's first settlers, and his father, Judge John Tyler, was a prominent Virginian statesman who "had the singular experience of presiding in the highest branches of each of the departments of state government" as speaker of the Virginia House of Delegates, judge on the Court of Appeals, and governor of Virginia.[1] The senior Tyler even made his mark during the ratification debates over the federal Constitution, serving as vice president of the Virginia ratifying convention and speaking against the Constitution as a vehement Anti-Federalist. Along with these political connections, Judge Tyler had personal relationships with the major figures of Virginia politics. He had been Thomas Jefferson's roommate at the College of William & Mary; served in the House of Delegates with James Madison and John Marshall; and was personal friends with James Monroe and Patrick Henry.[2]

With this background, it is unsurprising that the younger Tyler was groomed for a political career and given an education in the Jeffersonian tradition of strict constitutional interpretation, states' rights, and expansionism. These views were further entrenched during the young Tyler's time at William & Mary as his primary teacher, college president Bishop James Madison—cousin of the president of the same name—"sought to cultivate the Jeffersonian ideals of limited government and free trade in his students."[3] By the time he graduated in 1807, the young Tyler was inspired by "visions of national greatness and a belief in the

American republic's God-given destiny."⁴ Tyler carried these abstract ideas into his political career and attempted to apply them to the hard realities of practical politics.

The Congressman from Virginia

After graduating from William & Mary, Tyler studied law under his father and Edmund Randolph, the first United States attorney general and second secretary of state under George Washington. Admitted to the bar in 1809, Tyler soon left the law and turned to politics, being elected to the Virginia House of Delegates in 1811 and later serving on the Virginia governor's Council of State.

Yet an opportunity to step onto the national stage soon opened up for the young politician. When Congressman John Clopton died in September 1816, a special election was called to fill his seat. Running as a Jeffersonian Democratic-Republican, Tyler found himself in a hard-fought election against Virginia house speaker Andrew Stevenson, a fellow Democratic-Republican. Tyler won the election by only thirty votes in what his son Lyon Tyler called "a mere trial of personal popularity, as they fully concurred in political principle."⁵

Moving to Washington in December 1816, Tyler entered Congress during the period known as the "Era of Good Feelings," where the Democratic-Republicans' dominant supermajorities in Congress and the collapse of the opposition Federalist Party all but erased the divisive partisan conflicts which had characterized much of the United States' early history. Yet the Democratic-Republicans were not monolithic, and Tyler became associated with the conservative faction of the party known as the Old Republicans. This faction consisted primarily of southerners who emphasized "states' rights, opposition to a strong central government, and strict construction of the Constitution."⁶

The influence of this faction on Tyler's thinking was especially evident as the nation experienced its first sectional crisis over whether to admit Missouri to the Union. In February 1819, Representative James Tallmadge of New York proposed that Missouri's admittance be conditional upon its adoption of a gradual emancipation plan ending slavery and prohibiting the importation of slaves into the state. The debate over the Tallmadge proposal quickly deteriorated into a regional dispute, with northerners in support and southerners in opposition.[7]

Tyler himself was absent for most of the debate due to ill health but finally gave a speech regarding Missouri's entry on February 17, 1820, the day after the House linked the Tallmadge amendments to Missouri statehood. As noted by Dan Monroe, Tyler's Missouri speech attempted to refute a variety of arguments that had been offered by opponents of Missouri's entry, and as such "lacked a coherent narrative flow, resembling a hodge-podge of rhetoric tacked together by non-sequiturs."[8] Nonetheless, the speech grants us several insights into how Tyler viewed westward expansion, and in particular the role he saw slavery playing in that expansion.

First, we see Tyler maintained a strong commitment to the South and to states' rights. Despite opening his speech by decrying the sectionalism that had emerged in the debate, Tyler laid the blame for the crisis solely on "the work of the North, and not of the South."[9] Specifically, by attempting to place conditions on Missouri statehood, Northern congressmen had introduced an "unusual and extraordinary proposition" which threatened to abridge "the exercise of an essential right."[10] Most of Tyler's speech follows this central theme, as he argued that placing conditions on Missouri's entry was both an unconstitutional expansion of Congress' power and a violation of the fundamental principle of states' rights. For Tyler, Congress' only role in admitting new states was "to admit or refuse."[11] No other state had restrictions placed upon them for admission, and the proposed conditions interfered with Missourians' right to write their own constitution and laws. For Missouri to become a state under these circumstances would mean that "she is neither equal to [other states], nor, like them, is she sovereign."[12] Reflecting his commitment to a strict reading of the Constitution, Tyler insisted that if Congress wanted to be able to place conditions on becoming a state, a constitutional amendment would be required.[13]

Notably, while Tyler addressed the core issue of slavery, he declined to defend the peculiar institution itself. His most recent biographer, Christopher Leahy, contends that unlike many southerners, Tyler's opposition to the Missouri Compromise "did not serve as a proxy for the outright defense of slavery."[14] Rather, Tyler seems to have viewed slavery much as his hero Jefferson did: as an existing evil for which they did not currently have an answer, but which they hoped would one day be abolished. To that end, Tyler became the primary spokesperson in Congress for the theory of "diffusion." This idea, first articulated by Jefferson and Madison, held that slavery should be expanded into the territories as this would lower the slave populations in the slave states, making slavery less integral to society and abolition less costly.[15] For Tyler, allowing slavery into Missouri would serve just such a purpose. The institution's "dark cloud" would be reduced to "a summer's cloud." Moreover, the diffusion of slavery would "advance the interest, and secure the safety of one-half of this extended Republic . . . ameliorate the condition of the slave, and . . . add much to the prospects of emancipation and the total extinction of slavery."[16]

Tyler's speech opposing the conditional admission of Missouri demonstrates three important aspects of his political thought that would come into play during the annexation of Texas. First, it clearly shows Tyler to be a proponent of territorial expansion, with Edward Crapol contending that Tyler's arguments were typical of the "national greatness" ideology in foreign policy.[17] Second, in arguing for diffusion theory, we see Tyler's support for expanding slavery was not for the peculiar institution's own sake, but with the broader goals of eventually ending slavery—albeit counterintuitively—and easing nascent sectional tensions. Finally, it is indicative of Tyler's commitment to a Jeffersonian strict-constructionist interpretation of the Constitution, as he believed Congress did not have the constitutional authority to place conditions on entry into the Union.

The Missouri Crisis was ultimately resolved with a compromise forged by Speaker of the House Henry Clay. First, Missouri would be allowed to enter the Union as a slave state provided that Maine—then a part of Massachusetts—entered as a free state. Second, slavery would be banned in territories north of the 36° 30' latitude line but permitted in territories south of it.[18] Both measures passed Congress and were signed by President James Monroe. Tyler, however, voted against both.[19] Discouraged by the Missouri Compromise and dogged by lingering ill health, Tyler declined to seek reelection and left the House in 1821.

Senator Tyler and the Second Party System

Yet Tyler was not done with politics. By 1823, Tyler decided he had had enough of private life, and he successfully ran to reenter the Virginia House of Delegates. Tyler threw himself into the business of the legislature, but his aim was undoubtedly to gain higher office. At the time, US senators were elected by state legislatures, and Tyler's work led to him being considered for an open Senate seat in 1824. While he was ultimately passed over, in 1825 the legislature elected him governor of Virginia, the same office his father had held fifteen years earlier.

Given that the Virginia governorship was an office "of considerable dignity but of little power,"[20] Tyler's gubernatorial experience was fairly uneventful, his most notable act being his eulogy for Thomas Jefferson after the Sage of Monticello's death on July 4, 1826.[21] The next year, the legislature once again considered Tyler for a Senate seat, although this one was occupied by Tyler's old congressional colleague and ideological ally, the eccentric John Randolph of Roanoke. Randolph had served in Congress off and on since 1799, but with long political careers come enemies, and Randolph's volatile personality and tendency for outrageous behavior had earned him quite a few. Tyler dutifully feigned disinterest in the office, as was expected of politicians of the time, but he assured friends and allies that he would accept the seat if elected to it. This was enough for the Virginia legislature to send him back to Washington on a close vote of 115–110.[22]

Tyler did not face any major expansion issues during his time in the Senate, but he retained his grand vision of what he thought the United States could be. During a debate over a tariff bill in 1832, Tyler argued that the United States should embrace free trade as a way to gain prosperity and influence across the world. As part of an extensive speech delivered over the course of three days, Tyler provided a rhapsodic description of what he envisioned a future America to look like. Condemning tariff supporters as too parochial, Tyler declared that his

> imagination has led me to look into the distant future, and there to contemplate the greatness of free America. I have beheld her walking on the waves of the mighty deep, carrying along with her

tidings of great joy to distant nations. I have seen her overturning the strong places of despotism, and restoring to man his long-lost rights.[23]

Such a description clearly shows that Tyler was committed to further expansion, as only a powerful nation spanning a continent would be able to achieve the vision Tyler had for it.

While Tyler imagined a truly continental United States able to project its power around the globe, back in Washington the political situation was far more factious than it had been when Tyler was a young congressman. The one-party system of the Democratic-Republicans had broken down in the contentious presidential election of 1824 as four major candidates, Secretary of State John Quincy Adams, Secretary of the Treasury William Crawford, Speaker of the House Henry Clay, and General Andrew Jackson all vied for the presidency. In the end, none of the candidates won a majority in the Electoral College, sending the top three finishers, Jackson, Adams, and Crawford, to a contingent election in the House. Clay, meanwhile, was positioned to act as a kingmaker due to his immense influence over the House. As Crawford was known to have health problems—he had suffered a stroke in 1823—the contest came down to Jackson and Adams. Yet despite the fact that Jackson had won a plurality of the electoral and popular vote, when the House finished voting it was Adams who emerged victorious. When Adams then appointed Clay as his secretary of state, Jackson and his supporters accused them of striking a "corrupt bargain."[24]

The animosities that had animated the campaign continued after Adams was inaugurated. For his part, the new president hoped to continue the Era of Good Feelings, insisting that his "great object would be to break up the remnant of old party distinctions."[25] Jackson's supporters, however, had no interest in retaining the one-party system and organized themselves into a cohesive opposition. The driving force behind this movement was New York senator Martin Van Buren, who created a new, mass-based Democratic Party around Jackson. The Jacksonians' superior organization enabled them to win majorities in both houses of Congress in the 1826 elections.[26]

Tyler's elevation to the Senate was a part of this initial Jacksonian wave, and he remarked to a correspondent that with the "Jackson party" in control of Congress, "the opposition party constitute in fact the *administration*."[27] Despite aligning with the Jacksonians in the Senate, Tyler had previously been a critic of Jackson. During his first term in the House, Tyler had denounced the general for his military aggression in seizing Spanish Florida while fighting the indigenous Seminoles. Notably, Tyler did not object to the seizure of Florida itself—which was in line with his general approval of territorial expansion—but he argued that Jackson, a military officer, had usurped the powers of declaring war, annexing territory, appointing territorial officials, and establishing American law. In Tyler's view, such actions undermined the Constitution and created the potential for military despotism.[28]

The Virginian's antipathy for Jackson continued into the 1824 election as Tyler actively opposed Jackson's candidacy and supported Adams.[29] When Adams won, Tyler wrote to Clay thanking him for his role in resolving the election and disdainfully referred to Jackson as "a mere soldier" who had shown "little value as a civilian."[30]

Once in office, however, Adams laid out an ambitious nationalist agenda which Tyler saw as demonstrating "an almost disregard of the federative principle—a more latitudinous construction of the Constitution than ever before had been insisted on."[31] Thus, when Tyler entered the Senate, he joined with the Jacksonian Democrats in opposing the president, while remaining ambivalent about Jackson himself. In the 1828 election, he supported Jackson as the lesser of two evils, remarking to his brother-in-law that "Turning to him [Jackson] I may at least indulge in hope; looking on Adams I must despair."[32]

After Jackson defeated Adams and ascended to the presidency, he vindicated Tyler's hope by opposing internal improvements and fighting against the national bank, two issues Tyler had long viewed as unconstitutional. When Jackson vetoed the recharter of the national bank in 1832, Tyler "could only cheer."[33] Yet the senator was not an uncritical supporter of the president. On the contrary, Tyler criticized Jackson's spoils system which rewarded party officials with jobs in the federal bureaucracy. He also condemned what he considered to be Jackson's abuse of recess appointments as unconstitutional attempts to circumvent the Senate's role in the appointment process.[34] Despite these disagreements,

Tyler supported Jackson in the 1832 election against Clay and instructed his daughter to "speak of me always as a Jackson man whenever you are questioned."[35]

This request, however, proved to be premature, as Old Hickory's second term forced the Virginian to reconsider his partisan allegiance. Of particular concern was Jackson's reaction to the Nullification Crisis. This crisis emerged when South Carolina, led by Vice President John C. Calhoun, declared that it had the authority to nullify national laws it found unconstitutional and proceeded to nullify the Tariff of 1828. In response, Jackson pushed Congress to pass the Force Bill authorizing the president to use military force to bring the nullifiers back into line.[36]

For Tyler, there were two major problems with the bill. First, its focus on national supremacy over the states was at odds with Tyler's strong states' rights convictions. Second, it would substantially expand executive power. Tyler specifically criticized the sections allowing the president to deploy military force whenever there were "unlawful threats" to collecting revenue or any obstructions to federal law, as well as against any "aiders and abettors" of such activities. This language appeared overly broad to the Virginia senator, and he complained it could apply to nearly anything, even rhetorically asking if military force would be used against "a drunken blackguard in the streets" who happened to abuse a government inspector. Such measures and ambiguous language placed a large amount of discretion in the president to choose whether he would exercise military power not only against the states, but in the smallest cases of infringement. While Tyler claimed that he had "all proper confidence in the President," he reiterated his "instinctive abhorrence to confiding extravagant powers in the hands of any one man." He further expressed his fears that such a bill could set a harmful precedent for power-hungry officeholders in the future.[37]

Tyler's reaction to the Force Bill clearly shows his concerns about Jackson's aggressive use of presidential power. When Jackson later ordered his subordinates to remove federal funds from the national bank, it only solidified Tyler's break with him.[38] As Tyler had previously supported Jackson's actions against the bank, he now had to explain what had changed. In his speech criticizing Jackson's actions, Tyler did not focus on whether he thought the bank should cease to exist—he did—

but rather on how its extinction should come about. In his estimation, Jackson had already set the bank on the road to dissolution by vetoing its charter. To take the extra step of moving the deposits was, to Tyler, illegal, and he declared that "if it is to die, let it die by law." More seriously, Tyler argued that there was a separation of powers issue at play, as Congress, not the president, was charged with overseeing public funds. Indeed, the prospect of the president handling public funds seemed to disturb Tyler the most, as he warned that "money is more dangerous than armed men."[39] Tyler elaborated on his views in a letter to his brother-in-law, writing that "concede to the President the power to dispose of the public money as he pleases, and it is vain to talk of checker and balances."[40] When the Senate considered a resolution censuring the president for his actions, Tyler voted for it.

Combined with the Force Bill, the removal controversy served as the last straw for Tyler. At the end of his speech condemning Jackson's actions, he argued that the Democrats were merely a "party which changes its principles as the chameleon its color" and involved only in "President-making."[41] He then left the Democratic Party and joined the new opposition Whig Party. Having come together as a unified party only the previous year in 1833, the Whigs were a peculiar collection of disparate factions, but was generally composed of two groups: Southern strict constructionists—whom Tyler now identified with—and nationalists led by Clay and Massachusetts senator Daniel Webster. Such an alliance was undoubtedly odd. The nationalist wing was composed of advocates of Clay's "American System" of high tariffs, internal improvements, and a national bank, all things that Tyler and other Southern strict constructionists opposed. Their unity, at this stage, came solely from their distrust of executive power, particularly as exercised by Jackson. Yet the Whigs' ideological diversity was more a symptom of the party's "infancy and youth." Once it "reached maturity the qualities inherited from the National Republican party [of Clay and Webster] asserted an absolute dominance."[42] While that later proved to be a problem for Tyler, his initial conversion was considered a political coup by the Whigs, and they rewarded Tyler by electing him Senate president pro tempore.

Even as Tyler was honored by his new co-partisans, his party switch turned out to be a double-edged sword. In the short-term, the Democratic majority in the Virginia House of Delegates passed a resolution instructing Tyler to vote in favor of a resolution expunging Jackson's censure—which he had voted for initially—from the congressional record. This placed Tyler in a conundrum. He had long held that senators were agents of the state legislatures and bound to do the legislature's will in Congress. Yet he also considered the act of expunging material from the congressional record to be unconstitutional on the grounds that the Constitution requires each house to keep a journal.[43] To avoid violating his principles and ensure he did not disobey state instructions he felt duty-bound to respect, he resigned from the Senate on February 29, 1836.[44]

Taking Tyler's actions during the Jackson administration as a whole, we see that Tyler tended to have a limited conception of executive power. Yet he was not an advocate of complete executive subordination, having supported Jackson's bank veto and actions against internal improvements. This suggests that even while Tyler opposed robust executive power, he was not wholly in favor of the kind of legislative supremacy that some of his new Whig colleagues embraced.

Rise to National Prominence

Just like his first retirement from Congress, it would not be long before Tyler reentered politics. In the 1836 presidential election the Whigs attempted an unusual campaign strategy. Unable to unite their disparate factions behind a single candidate against Jackson's handpicked successor, Vice President Martin Van Buren, they ran four candidates focused on different states and regions: Daniel Webster in Massachusetts, North Carolina senator Willie Person Mangum in South Carolina, General William Henry Harrison in the North and border states, and Tennessee senator Hugh Lawson White in the South. With so many candidates, the Whigs hoped to make up for their lack of organization and allow candidates the flexibility to make sectional appeals. The implied goal, however, seemed to be to deny Van Buren an Electoral College majority and throw the election to the House.[45] Tyler, despite being new to the party, was nominated as the vice presidential candidate by the Whigs in Maryland, South Carolina, Georgia, and Tennessee, becoming the running mate of three out of the four candidates: Harrison, White, and Mangum.[46]

While Van Buren handily defeated all four of his opponents, Tyler's position on the tickets cemented his status as a major national figure in the Whig Party, particularly among states' rights southerners. This status would come into play as the Whigs considered who to put on their ticket for the 1840 election. By this point, Tyler had become a strong Clay supporter, telling the Kentucky senator in September 1839 of the "great solicitude" he felt for Clay's "elevation to the Presidency."[47] When the Whigs gathered for their national convention a few months later, Tyler attended as a Clay delegate.

Tyler's public support for Clay soon redounded to his advantage. For despite receiving a plurality in the early rounds of voting, Clay was twenty-five votes short of the majority necessary to clinch the nomination.[48] After several ballots and much political maneuvering, William Henry Harrison, a famous general nicknamed "Tippecanoe" in reference to one of his battles, emerged as the victor. Yet Harrison's nomination left two groups in the Whig coalition unsatisfied: southerners and Clay supporters. Thus, when the convention turned to the vice presidential nominee, it looked for someone who could simultaneously satisfy both groups, ultimately settling on Tyler. As a Virginian, he could represent the Southern Whigs on the ticket, and "his zealous and untiring efforts to procure [Clay's] nomination for the presidency" satisfied Clay supporters that their concerns would not be overlooked.[49] Leaning into Harrison's military credentials, the pair ran under the catchy alliterative slogan "Tippecanoe and Tyler, Too."

The Accidental President

The election of 1840 was a stunning repudiation of Van Buren and the Democrats. In an election that saw the highest voter turnout of any presidential election to that point—80.2 percent—the Harrison-Tyler ticket won a dominant Electoral College majority of 234 to 60. Additionally, the Whigs won large majorities in both houses of Congress.[50] It was the first—and ultimately last—time that the Whigs would have unified control of government.

The Whigs' political fortunes began to decline almost as soon as Harrison took office. Disagreements over cabinet and patronage appointments led to a major rift between Harrison and Clay which could have split the party. But before those disagreements could spill over to the rest of the party, Harrison fell ill with pneumonia. After suffering for several days, Harrison died. He had been president for exactly one month.[51]

As the first president to die in office, Harrison's death shocked the nation. Tyler—who had been at his home in Williamsburg, Virginia during Harrison's month in office—rushed back to Washington when he heard the news. Once there, he asserted that he was now the president of the United States. Yet the constitutional text was not so clear on that point. Article II, Section 1 of the Constitution merely stated that "the Powers and Duties" of the presidency "shall devolve on the Vice President" in the event of a vacancy.[52] This left open the question of whether the thing devolving on the vice president referred to the office itself or merely its powers. Following the latter interpretation would make Tyler simply the acting president for the remainder of the term, while the former would make Tyler fully *the president*. While a seemingly minor distinction, the difference between being the president and being an acting president could have major ramifications for how Tyler utilized the office. By fully becoming president, Tyler would have more independence in how he employed the office's authority. If he was only the acting president, there likely would be institutional pressure—both from popular opinion and from Congress and Harrison's cabinet—to be a caretaker, attempting to carry out the policies of the late president rather than forging his own policy agenda.[53]

Despite the uncertainty, Tyler was unequivocal that he was the president, "assuming the office's powers in toto."[54] He moved immediately into the White House and had himself sworn in by William Cranch, chief justice of the Circuit Court of the District of Columbia. Interestingly, Cranch noted that Tyler "deem[ed] himself qualified" and able to assume the office without a second oath, and that the new president only took the oath out of a sense of "greater caution" and to preempt any "doubts [that] may arise."[55] Congressional Whigs also came to Tyler's aid by directly countering challenges to the new president's legitimacy and passing a resolution to address Tyler as president.[56] These actions set the precedent that the vice president would become the president in the event of a vacancy, and the Tyler Precedent guided presidential succession until it was codified into the Twenty-Fifth Amendment in 1967.[57]

Such actions did not, however, entirely quell the lingering whispers of Tyler's illegitimacy. John Quincy Adams—now a congressman from Massachusetts—contended that the strict constructionist Tyler exceeded his powers and violated his own principles in assuming the office, writing that "a strict constructionist would warrant more than a doubt whether the Vice-President has a right to occupy the President's house, or to claim his salary, without an Act of Congress." The former president went on to say that "Vice-President acting as President . . . would be the correct style."[58] Clay similarly continued to refer to Tyler variously as the vice president or "acting president" in his correspondence.[59] More derisively, Tyler's opponents gave him the mocking nickname of "His Accidency."

Yet beyond remarking in his assumption address that it was the first time the office had "devolved" upon the vice president, Tyler said little publicly about his transition to the presidency.[60] He passively ignored the little indignities of nicknames, with his most active refutation being the return of a package addressed to the "Acting President."[61] The only time Tyler appears to have truly engaged with this question on a serious level was in his first meeting with the late president's cabinet.

Whig Party doctrine held that the cabinet should act as a kind of intra-executive check on the president to prevent the accumulation of executive power. During Harrison's brief tenure, this doctrine emerged in the cabinet's insistence on deciding issues by majority vote, with the president's vote having the same value as each of the cabinet secretaries. Harrison had begun to chafe against this model during his month in office, yet it was still in place when he died.[62] Upon being informed of this procedure by Secretary of State Daniel Webster, Tyler is reported to have replied that he could "never consent to being dictated as to what I shall or shall not do. I, as President, shall be responsible for my administration."[63] He informed the cabinet members that if they disagreed, they were free to resign.

Such assertiveness against Whig doctrine served as a portent of things to come. While his first message as president hit on Whig themes about limiting executive patronage and the president's removal power, as well as the importance of maintaining a "complete separation ... between the sword and the purse," Tyler was ambiguous about major items of the Whig's economic agenda, such as the national bank and tariffs.[64] In his message to the special session of Congress that Harrison had called before his death, Tyler sent conflicting signals, informing Congress that he did not wish to disturb "the patriotic desires of the late President," yet also elaborating his own policy goals. Similarly, he struck the tone of a Whig president who would defer to Congress, yet also claimed "the ultimate power of rejecting any measure which may, in my view of it, conflict with the Constitution or otherwise jeopardize the prosperity of the country."[65] For Whigs anxious to use their new congressional majorities to enact Clay's American System of high tariffs, internal improvements, and a national bank, it was hard to know where Tyler stood. Clay himself remarked to a correspondent that even though "the best and most amicable relations exist[ed]" between himself and Tyler, he could "only conjecture" about what the new president would do.[66]

That ambiguity was soon resolved by Tyler vetoing two bills passed by Congress to create a new national bank, reiterating his consistent opposition to the national bank and his Jeffersonian belief that it was unconstitutional.[67] The reaction from Clay and the Whigs was swift. Two days after the second veto, Clay orchestrated an elaborate performance whereby Tyler's cabinet members individually presented their resignations to Tyler over the course of five hours. Only Webster remained, most likely due to his own rivalry with Clay.[68] That night, the congressional Whigs met and went even further, expelling Tyler from the party and insisting they "can be no longer, in any manner or degree, justly held responsible or blamed for the administration of the executive branch of the government."[69] Tyler had become "an anomaly of presidential history: a president without a party."[70]

Abandoned by the Whigs and distrusted by the Democrats, Tyler was in a difficult and politically isolated position. Yet the resignation of Harrison's cabinet did afford him the opportunity to regain some control of his administration as he appointed replacements who were more ideologically aligned with him, paying particular attention to states' rights Whigs who "were Jackson men in the beginning and who fell off from his administration."[71]

Nonetheless, even with his own appointees, Tyler still found himself stymied by a Whig Congress who looked on him not simply as a president with whom they had policy differences, but as an apostate. It was at this low point in October 1841 that Tyler turned to one policy he had consistently supported his entire career. In his first speech to Congress several months earlier, the new president highlighted his support of American expansion "to reclaim our almost illimitable wilderness." While he did not mention Texas or any other territory explicitly, he asserted that the federal system would enable "the greatest expansion."[72] In the first few months of his unexpected term, Tyler had put his expansionist ambitions to the side as he fought with the Whigs over economic issues. Now, without a party and facing an obstinate Congress, Tyler saw territorial expansion as a way to revitalize his flailing administration and save his presidency. Writing to Webster, he asked the secretary of state, "Would any thing [sic] throw so bright a lustre [sic] on us" as the acquisition of Texas?[73]

CHAPTER 3

Sam Houston and the Republic of Texas

It is unsurprising that Tyler, desperate for a political victory, would look to Texas as the solution to his administration's woes. Americans had been interested in the territory since at least the Louisiana Purchase in 1803. As the southwestern boundary of Louisiana was left largely undefined by the purchase, some Americans—including President Thomas Jefferson—argued that Louisiana extended down to the Rio Grande, encompassing "all of Texas."[1] While such arguments did not translate to actual control over the territory, these claims persisted, and became a major point of contention sixteen years later during the negotiations over the Adams-Onís Treaty in 1819. In those talks, then secretary of state John Quincy Adams repeatedly pressed the United States' claim to Texas. Spain, however, refused to concede, and the resulting treaty saw the United States cede its claims to Texas in exchange for acquiring Florida and the entirety of the Gulf coast east of the Mississippi River.[2]

Yet this concession did not deter many Americans from envisioning Texas as a future state. Writing over a year after the Adams-Onís Treaty was signed, Jefferson predicted that "Techas [sic] will be the richest state of our union," and told President James Monroe that far from diminishing American claims to Texas, the treaty actually had "the valuable effect of strengthening our title to Techas [sic]" as the exchange "imports an acknowledgement of our right to it."[3] Other Americans were not so sanguine about Texas' future in the Union as Jefferson, and believed that the treaty had "unjustly deprived" the United States of territory.[4] In order to right this perceived wrong, some expansionists attempted to dislodge Texas from Spain themselves. These private military expeditions, known as "filibusters"—derived from the Spanish *filibustero* for "freebooter"[5]—were undertaken by enterprising Americans, typically from the South, with surprising frequency during the antebellum period, despite violating American and international law. Prior to the Civil War, American filibusterers made expeditions into Canada, Mexico, Ecuador, Honduras, and Cuba.[6]

Texas was the site of several failed filibuster campaigns, the two most notable being the Gutiérrez-Magee Expedition in 1811–1812 and the Long Filibuster in 1819. The Gutiérrez-Magee Expedition was a joint effort of American Army officer Augustus Magee and Mexican revolutionary Bernardo Gutiérrez de Lara. While Magee and Gutiérrez successfully defeated a Spanish army and captured a Spanish general, the filibuster soon broke down from internal dissension and ended with both Magee and Gutiérrez dead and their followers executed.[7] The Long Expedition, led by US Army surgeon James Long, was undertaken in direct response to the Adams-Onís Treaty in 1819 and succeeded in seizing the city of Nacogdoches and declaring Texas to be an independent republic. Unfortunately for Long, this success was fleeting. The Spanish soon reclaimed Nacogdoches and drove the filibusterer back to American soil.[8]

When Spain finally lost Texas, it was due not to the actions of filibustering Anglo-Americans, but to the efforts of Mexican revolutionaries. In 1821, Mexico won its independence from Spain following a bloody eleven-year war. Yet it took a few more years to determine Texas' precise role in the new Mexican system. Initially, the Mexican government continued to view Texas as part of the inherited Provincias Internas, a Spanish imperial district that covered northern Mexico and what eventually became the southwestern United States from California to Texas. It was not until the implementation of the Mexican constitution of 1824 that Texas was united with Coahuila as the official Mexican state of "Coahuila y Tejas."[9]

Texas' shift from Spain to Mexico reignited the imaginations of Americans eager to expand into the southwest. The new Mexican government itself fueled the dreams of expansionists by enabling and encouraging American settlement, offering large land grants to individuals—known as *empresarios*—who could settle at least two hundred families in Mexico within a certain period of time. In addition to land, immigrants would receive tax breaks and tariff privileges. The only requirement placed on new arrivals was that they be Roman Catholic or convert to Catholicism within three years of immigrating.[10] *Empresarios* like Stephen F. Austin—who would later be hailed as the "Father of Texas"—moved thousands of families into Mexican Texas.[11] By the time the Texas Revolution broke out in October 1835, the non-indigenous population of Texas had exploded to roughly forty thousand, many of them from the Southern United States.[12] American immigration to Texas was so intense that by 1830, "Anglos in Texas outnumbered Hispanic *tejanos* more than two to one."[13]

At the same time, two successive American administrations anticipated that their newly independent neighbor might be more amenable to giving up Texas than Spain had been and offered to purchase the territory. The first attempt came under now-President John Quincy Adams, notably with the support of Secretary of State Henry Clay. Soon after taking office in March 1825, Adams appointed Joel R. Poinsett as the first American minister to Mexico. An experienced diplomat, Poinsett had served as a special agent to South America during the Madison administration before serving two terms in the House of Representatives.[14] As minister to Mexico, Poinsett astutely determined that "the administration simply did not understand the intensity of Mexican feelings on the matter" and believed that an offer to purchase Texas would be seen as both "unpersuasive [and] insulting."[15] Instead, Poinsett negotiated the first Mexican-American treaty establishing that the boundaries between the two nations would be the same as those which had been set in the Adams-Onís Treaty, with Texas remaining in Mexico.[16]

After Jackson defeated Adams and became president in 1829, one of his first actions was to inquire about acquiring Texas. The new chief executive believed the concession of Texas in the Adams-Onís Treaty had been a mistake and sought rectify it. Moreover, Jackson saw the purchase of Texas as necessary for both western expansion and national security, declaring in a letter to Secretary of State Martin Van Buren that holding Texas was "necessary for the security of the great emporium of the west" and critical for controlling the Mississippi River valley. Jackson further informed Van Buren that he would make an initial offer of

$3 million for Texas, but would go as high as $5 million.[17] Unfortunately for Jackson, while his emissary Anthony Butler made the offer to Mexico, he was unable to secure a deal before Texas itself broke out in revolt.[18] Once the Texas Revolution began, the politics of annexation—both domestically and internationally—became much more complicated, particularly after the Texians established themselves as an independent republic led by President Sam Houston.

"The Raven": Sam Houston

Sam Houston was born on March 2, 1793, on the Virginia frontier to a family of moderate means which owned a plantation in the Shenandoah Valley. While not a blue-blood family like the Tylers, Houston's father, Captain Samuel Houston, had served in an elite unit of riflemen during the Revolutionary War, and the Houstons were well-regarded among their neighbors. But when the elder Houston died in 1807 leaving the family with substantial debts, the family sold the plantation and moved west.[19]

Settling in eastern Tennessee, the Houstons established a farm and opened up a store, regaining some of the wealth that they had lost in Virginia. The fifth of six sons, young Sam Houston had little interest in agricultural or mercantile pursuits, being much more interested in his late father's considerable library. Discontented with working in the family business—as well as with his formal education at a local school—Houston ran away from home at the age of sixteen. Coming across a Cherokee village, he was taken in by their leader Oolooteka, whose name meant "Man-who-beats-his-own-drum," and who was known to white settlers as "John Jolly."[20] Adopted as a son by Oolooteka, Houston was given the name "Colonneh," Cherokee for "the Raven," a symbol of good luck and wandering in Cherokee mythology.[21]

After living with the Cherokee for three years, Houston enlisted in the US Army in 1813 and was immediately promoted to sergeant. Enlisting in the middle of the War of 1812 with Great Britain, Houston's unit was assigned to the southwestern frontier to fight Native Americans who had sided with the British, particularly the Creeks. Houston distinguished himself during the campaign and made lasting connections with men who later enabled his political career, most notably General Andrew Jackson, who began treating the fellow Tennessean as his protégé.

Leaving the army in 1818, Houston began reading law and opened a legal practice in Tennessee. Like Tyler, however, it was not long before Houston left the law for politics. Tennessee's population was booming, and the state gained three new congressional seats as a result of the 1820 census. With encouragement from Jackson and Tennessee governor Joseph McMinn, Houston ran as a Democratic-Republican for the newly created Ninth District and—due to behind-the-scenes machinations by Jackson and McMinn—was unopposed.[22]

As a freshman congressman in 1823, Houston did not make much of an impact. In an era where the House was the venue for the stunning oratory of Daniel Webster, Henry Clay, and John Randolph of Roanoke, Houston largely kept quiet, addressing the House only once in his first term to support recognizing the Greeks in their war for independence against the Ottoman Empire. Yet in that speech he foreshadowed his career as a revolutionary and practiced arguments he would later employ when advocating for the United States to recognize Texas. Dismissing concerns that American recognition might lead to a war between the United States and the Ottomans, Houston urged his fellow congressmen to "hail [the Greeks] as brethren and cheer them in their struggle."[23] Noting the recent precedent of the United States recognizing the newly independent republics of Latin America,[24] Houston insisted that the consistent principle of American foreign policy had been to "extend a helping hand, like men" towards "a people that held the strongest claims upon us."[25] Houston's speech also demonstrated a Jacksonian trust in executive power—or at least trust in President James Monroe—arguing that the resolution should be passed to illustrate "confidence" in the president's judgment, as the executive is constitutionally granted authority over diplomatic recognition.[26] With this short speech, Houston not only illustrated his belief in the universality of American principles and in the United States' diplomatic responsibility to encourage nations fighting for their independence, but he also showed his support for executive power and discretion in foreign policy.

It was also during his time in the House that Houston's position as a

Jacksonian fully crystallized, both in his commitment to Jackson's personal political fortunes and in adhering to an ideology that emphasized popular sovereignty. As mentioned in the previous chapter, the presidential election of 1824 saw all four candidates fail to win a majority in the Electoral College, throwing the election to the House. While there were no debates in the House over the contingent election, Houston vigorously supported Jackson as the only legitimate choice, telling a correspondent that Jackson "is certainly the President of the People."[27] When Jackson lost to Adams, Houston published a circular letter to his constituents bemoaning

> a manifest defect in the Constitution in relation to the election of the President . . . The individual who was manifestly the choice of the majority of the people was not elevated to that distinguished situation for which his qualifications so pre-eminently fitted him . . . Another was chosen by the House of Representatives who had in his favor less expressions of national confidence, as manifested in the Electoral Colleges."[28]

Such rhetoric demonstrates not only that Houston retained a personal loyalty to Jackson, but also that he embraced the Jacksonian emphasis on popular sovereignty as the preeminent principle in government. As the personal antagonism between Jackson and Adams developed into a new party system, Houston assumed the role of Jackson's chief lieutenant in Washington, with Jackson's other protégés "deferring to Houston as the first among equals."[29]

Houston's status as Jackson's favored deputy was solidified when—with Old Hickory's backing—he was elected governor of Tennessee in 1827. When Jackson won the presidency a year later, it appeared that Houston was "Jackson's anointed successor-heir apparent to the Presidency of the United States."[30] Personal difficulties, however, soon derailed the young politician's steady rise to prominence. Houston had a reputation as a ladies' man, but in 1829 he decided to settle down and married Eliza Allen, the niece of one of Houston's friends in Congress and a woman sixteen years his junior. Within eleven weeks, the marriage fell apart, with Eliza leaving Houston. The reasons for why the marriage failed remain a mystery—neither Houston nor Eliza ever spoke of it[31]—

but the immediate result was the end of Houston's political career. The day after Eliza left, he resigned the governorship and returned to live with Oolooteka and the Cherokee, who by this point had been forced to move to the Arkansas Territory.

This second stint with the Cherokee lasted for three years, during which time Houston gained tribal citizenship and began acting as an agent of the Cherokee, representing them in dealings with the Jackson administration. In 1832, the former governor was convinced to join the growing wave of immigration to Texas, and he crossed the Red River into the Mexican state on December 2, 1832, settling in Nacogdoches.

Once there, Houston found his political fortunes revived. Within a few months of arriving Houston was called to represent his new home in the Convention of 1833 which petitioned the Mexican government for a redress of grievances, particularly related to making Tejas a distinct state and opposing laws which prohibited immigration from the United States and enforced Mexico's abolition of slavery among the new American arrivals. As noted in chapter one, Houston chaired the committee which drafted and proposed a new state constitution.

While the Mexican government eventually addressed some of these concerns, relations between the Texians and the national government in Mexico City continued to deteriorate.[32] They finally reached a breaking point in 1835 when the Mexican Congress repealed the constitution of 1824, destroying the federalist system Mexico had been operating under and replacing it with a unitary, centralized government.[33] The repeal "was the spark that ignited the province of Texas."[34] The Texians soon elected a Consultation to coordinate the response, and Houston was once again called upon to represent Nacogdoches.[35]

By the time a quorum assembled for the Consultation the fighting had already started, as a minor skirmish between Texian militia and Mexican cavalry in Gonzales, Texas was hailed as "the Lexington of Texas," equating it with the battle that launched the American Revolution.[36] Yet even with Texian troops in the field, the precise goals of the Revolution were unclear. Ultimately, the Consultation took a moderate approach so as not to alienate any potential supporters in Texas or among the Mexican opponents to the central government. It did not outright declare independence, but instead formed a provisional government with a governor, lieutenant governor, and council, asserting that the Texians were focused on affirming their natural rights and reestablishing the 1824 constitution. In response to the military situation, Houston was promoted to major general and given command of "the armies of Texas."[37]

The Consultation governed Texas for the next several months until a new convention was called in March 1836. This convention did declare independence and drafted a national constitution for the new Republic of Texas. Houston attended and even made the motion to adopt the declaration of independence, with its formal adoption coming on his birthday, March 2.[38] On March 4, Houston was confirmed as "Commander in Chief of all the land forces of the Texian Army," which included the interesting grant of being "endowed with all the rights, privileges and powers due to a Commander in chief in the United States of America."[39] With this appointment, Houston left to meet his army before the convention concluded.

Unfortunately for Houston, the war effort was not going well. The Alamo fell on March 6 to an army personally commanded by Mexican President Antonio López de Santa Anna. An experienced general, Santa Anna had used his military career to propel him to the summit of Mexican politics, becoming president after forcing his predecessor to resign and calling a new election, which he won easily. After repealing the constitution of 1824, Santa Anna personally put down several other uprisings that erupted at the same time as the one in Texas, most notably in the central Mexican state of Zacatecas, where the president allowed his soldiers to loot and plunder the state capital after defeating the rebels there. Santa Anna's decision to give no quarter to the defenders of the Alamo further cemented his reputation among the Texians as a ruthless tyrant.[40] Following the fall of the Alamo, a series of defeats afflicted the Texian cause. Houston was not present at these other battles, but the losses, along with his own troops' lack of discipline and shortage of supplies, convinced him to steadily retreat, precipitating the mass evacuation of Texians before the Mexican army now known as the "Runaway Scrape."[41]

Finally, on April 21, 1836, the Texians saw their fortunes completely reverse. Capturing intelligence that revealed Santa Anna and a small number of troops to be close by, Houston went on the offensive. In the ensuing Battle of San Jacinto—which only lasted roughly eighteen minutes—the Texians routed the Mexican force and captured Santa Anna. Houston had his horse shot out from under him and his ankle shattered by a stray bullet, leading the Mexican president to famously surrender to the Texian commander in chief while the latter lay on a blanket under an oak tree.[42] With Santa Anna as his prisoner, Houston and other Texian leaders were able to force substantial concessions, leading to the Treaty of Velasco, which required Santa Anna to order the withdrawal of Mexican forces. While the Mexican Senate never ratified the agreement, the Texians proclaimed victory, interpreting the Treaty of Velasco as ending the revolution and granting them their independence.[43]

The end of fighting meant the Texians could now turn to putting their new republic into operation. The first national Texas elections were held on September 5, 1836, and voters were asked not only to choose their elected officials, but also whether to ratify the 1836 constitution and if Texas should be annexed by the United States.[44] For much of the campaign, Houston was not even in the new country, having been taken to New Orleans to treat his wounds from San Jacinto. In his absence, the frontrunner for the presidency was undoubtedly Stephen Austin. The *empresario* had been at the forefront of Texas politics for over a decade and an essential part of the revolution. Henry Smith, who had served as governor under the provisional government of the Consultation, also was a candidate. Yet in Texas' nascent political environment the "emphasis was on personalities rather than principles," and no one had a bigger personality or following than Sam Houston.[45] It was, therefore, no surprise that when the general finally returned to Texas in early fall he crushed the other candidates in a landslide, winning the presidency with 79 percent of the vote.

The runaway dubbed "the Raven" had accomplished a feat more reminiscent of the mythical phoenix. Rising from the ashes of a political career destroyed by a failed marriage, Houston had turned his political exile into an opportunity, becoming the Hero of San Jacinto and the conqueror of Santa Anna. Instead of being Jackson's protégé and potential heir, Houston was now Jackson's equal, the president and head of state of an independent American-style republic.

Fighting for Recognition

Even more important than Houston's own election, however, were the results of the referenda on annexation and the 1836 constitution, both of which were overwhelmingly approved.[46] In his inaugural address, Houston acknowledged that "with a unanimity unparalleled" the Texians had "declared that they will be reunited to the great Republican family of the North" and committed his administration to annexation.[47] Thus, his election as president was not an unqualified endorsement to pursue whatever political program he wished, but came with a mandate on the issue central to the new republic's very existence. Of course, Houston personally supported annexation, telling a correspondent a month after being inaugurated to "by all means get Texas annexed to the U. States."[48] But even if he had not supported annexation, the immense support of the referendum would have likely required some action towards that goal.

Yet while Houston was bound by the Texians' popular will, the Americans were not, and it soon became evident that neither annexation nor even formal diplomatic recognition would be easily forthcoming. The American president alone had the constitutional authority to recognize other nations, and Jackson, despite his close relationship with Houston, did not immediately embrace his former disciple's new government.

On a personal level, Jackson wanted to annex Texas, seeing the region "as an essential component of his dream of empire,"[49] but from his vantage point as president he perceived major reasons both domestically and internationally for why it was not the right time to even recognize the young republic. Domestically, Texas was already becoming a source of conflict in the burgeoning tensions between Northern free states and Southern slave states. Southerners largely supported both recognition and annexation while Northerners opposed both. Some Northern abolitionists even argued that the entire Texas Revolution was nothing more than a plot by American slaveholders "to wrest the large and valuable territory of Texas from the Mexican Republic, in order to re-establish the SYSTEM OF SLAVERY; to open a vast and profitable SLAVE-MARKET therein; and, ultimately, to annex it to the United States."[50] On top of this sectional divide, Jackson saw that the Texas issue could divide the Democratic Party. Given that 1836 was an election year, with Jackson's hand-picked successor Vice President Martin Van Buren running for the presidency, Jackson viewed the prospect of inflaming the country by opening up a debate on Texas as not only detrimental to sectional harmony, but immensely damaging politically.[51]

Similarly, the international situation was tenuous. Santa Anna had been defeated and captured, but the treaty he signed at Velasco was not considered valid by the Mexican government due to the defeated president's status as a prisoner. When Santa Anna reached out to Jackson during his captivity asking the American president to mediate a new peace settlement, Old Hickory demurred, citing his general policy of non-intervention and the Mexican government's notice that "so long as [Santa Anna] is a prisoner, no act of [his] will be regarded as binding by Mexican authorities."[52]

In a special message to Congress on December 21, 1836, Jackson reiterated his insistence that the stated policy of the United States was "to avoid all interference in disputes which merely relate to the internal government of other nations," clearly suggesting that there were enough lingering uncertainties surrounding Texas, even after San Jacinto, that he considered it an internal Mexican issue. Indeed, it appeared to be only a matter of time before Mexico "rall[ied] its forces under a new leader and menac[ed] a fresh invasion to recover its lost dominion." The president did, however, highlight Texas' unique relationship with the United States, acknowledging not only that it had once been claimed as American territory but also that many of the Texians were

> emigrants from the United States, speak the same language with ourselves, cherish the same principles, political and religious, and are bound to many of our citizens by ties of friendship and kindred blood; and, more than all, it is known that the people of that country have instituted the same form of government with our own.

Jackson even noted that annexation was intimately bound with recognition, as the Texians "have . . . openly resolved, on the acknowledgment by us of their independence, to seek admission into the Union as one of the Federal States." Despite these considerations, Jackson declined to take a firm position, instead commenting that "prudence" dictated the United States "stand aloof" until either Mexico or another great power recognized Texas' claims, or Texas "proved beyond cavil or dispute" that it could maintain its independence.[53]

Jackson's message shocked the Texians. The president had supported Texas' inclusion in the Union for decades, having insisted that Texas was included in the Louisiana Purchase and viewing the cession of those claims in the Adams-Onís Treaty as a betrayal of American interests. Moreover, he had attempted to buy Texas himself only a few years before. Houston in particular was dumbfounded, telling a correspondent "How the U. States can get over our recognition, I can not conceive." Comparing Texas' position to that of the Central and South American republics, he argued that "None of the S. American States ever had higher claims, and surely Mexico, to the present moment has not fairer claims to recognition.[54]

Yet after delivering his message and—more importantly—after Van Buren won the presidential election, Jackson resumed his prior position of being much more open to both recognition and annexation. When Santa Anna was eventually released by the Texians, he traveled to Washington to meet with Jackson, where the two discussed the possibility of purchasing Texas.[55] While the idea ultimately went nowhere, the tide began turning in favor of Texas. On February 28, the House of Representatives included a provision in an appropriations bill that would fund an American minister to Texas whenever the president recognized the republic.[56] The Senate passed its own resolution pushing for recognition the next day, with the vote notably falling along sectional lines rather than party lines, with southerners in support and northerners in opposition.[57] Finally, in his last act as president, Jackson formally granted diplomatic recognition to the Republic of Texas on March 3, 1837, a year and a day after Texas declared independence.[58]

Annexation Stalls

Having finally been welcomed into the family of nations by his old mentor, Houston set to work convincing his fellow Jackson protégé and American counterpart Van Buren to take the next step and turn the

Lone Star Republic into the Lone Star State. Yet even while Van Buren had worked to purchase Texas as Jackson's secretary of state, he had refrained from coming out in support of either recognition or annexation during the 1836 campaign.[59] Once he became president, he remained hesitant, concerned about the effect Texas' addition would have on the sectional politics of the Union and on the Democratic Party.

In August 1837, Texas' new minister to Washington, Memucan Hunt Jr., formally proposed an annexation plan to American Secretary of State John Forsyth. When it was presented to Van Buren and the rest of the cabinet, the new president rejected the offer. In doing so, the Van Buren administration raised two issues. The first was the constitutional question of the procedure by which the United States might annex an independent nation. All the territory added by the United States up that point—specifically Louisiana and Florida—had been colonial possessions of other powers. What Texas was proposing, the subsuming of an independent republic into the United States, was a different issue altogether.[60] Ironically, Texas' success in achieving recognition had only served to introduce a new constitutional complication to the ultimate goal of annexation.

The other reason was more familiar, that the United States did not want to endanger its relationship with Mexico by admitting Texas. Even at this early stage, it was well understood that adding Texas to the American Union would almost certainly provoke war with Mexico, which still claimed Texas to be a part of its union.[61] The unspoken reason, however, remained Van Buren's desire to preserve sectional balance. This was partially for his own self-interest. Van Buren had formed the Democratic Party in the 1820s as an alliance of "the planters of the South and the plain Republicans of the north,"[62] and that connection remained central to the Democratic coalition. Thus to Van Buren, peace—within the party, between the sections, and with Mexico—all required a rejection of annexation.[63] That sectional politics was the true reason for Van Buren's rejection was guessed at by some of the Texians, with Texas Attorney General Peter Grayson remarking that "both parties here are afraid to move in the matter for fear of loosing [sic] popularity in the North."[64]

Undeterred, Hunt turned his attention to Congress, expressing the hope that one of the houses would pass a resolution directing the president to explore the possibilities of annexation.⁶⁵ Unfortunately for the Texians, this too proved to be futile. When a resolution was proposed in May 1838 supporting annexation, it was quickly derailed and bogged down in debate. Most notably, Adams—now a member of the House— had completely changed his views on Texas from when he was president.⁶⁶ Bogarting the House floor every morning from June 16 to July 7, the Massachusetts congressman conducted a one-man filibuster against annexation for three weeks. Living up to his nickname "Old Man Eloquent," Adams harangued the House and presented the abolitionist view that Texas annexation was nothing more than an effort to expand and entrench slavery. Due partially to Adams' efforts, the resolution failed, and along with it any hope of pushing annexation through Congress.⁶⁷

These difficulties led some in the Texas Congress to want to abandon annexation altogether. On April 23, 1838, Representative Anson Jones of Brazoria introduced a resolution stating that despite the people "express[ing] an almost unanimous desire to become annexed to the United States of North America," the United States' refusal led the Texians to "no longer desire such annexation," and authorizing the president to withdraw Texas' annexation proposal. Moreover, Jones's resolution proclaimed that further efforts toward annexation were limiting Texas' ability to move forward, particularly as the uncertainty was causing other powers to not formally recognize Texas. For Jones and supporters of the resolution, Texas had long since "demonstrated her ability for self government," and it was time for Texas to assert itself as an independent power without continually looking back towards the United States.⁶⁸ That the resolution failed by only a single vote, 14–13, illustrates not only the Texians' growing frustration with the inability to secure annexation, but also suggests that the idea of a permanently independent Texas was gaining support. After Congress adjourned in October 1838, Houston resigned himself to the fact that annexation would not be achieved while Van Buren was in the White House. Although dispatches from Washington repeatedly insisted that Van Buren supported annexation,⁶⁹ the divisive sectional politics of the time ensured no further action would be taken. As summarized by Hunt, "The measure is utterly impracticable under existing circumstances."⁷⁰ Appointing Jones as the new minister to Washington, Houston instructed him to withdraw the annexation offer in an attempt to save face and avoid the international humiliation of being turned down yet again.[71]

Despite failing to garner American support for annexation, Houston's constitutional authority positioned him to be the primary director of Texian foreign policy, enabling him to pursue alternative avenues of diplomatic support and ensure that his new government was not solely reliant on the United States for its continued existence. In June 1837 Houston had appointed James Pinckney Henderson—at the time serving as secretary of state—to act as Texas' minister to both Great Britain and France. If the United States would not bring Texas into the fold, then Houston hoped that recognition from major European powers might either put pressure on the Americans to change their minds or help safeguard Texas' future longevity. Unfortunately for Houston, nothing came of these efforts while he was in office. After several months lobbying the British government to recognize the young republic, Henderson was informed in December 1837 that the British had doubts about Texas' ability to "maintain its independence" and would refrain from recognition.[72] Henderson's initial efforts in France fared little better, as the French declined to recognize Texas until after an agent of the French legation inspected the nation and wrote a report on its prospects.[73] These efforts did, however, bear fruit after Houston left office, as Henderson secured a treaty with France that officially recognized Texas' independence on September 25, 1839.[74]

Nonetheless, the failure to secure annexation to the United States and the struggle to gain international recognition during his administration hung over Houston as he prepared to leave office in December 1838. As the constitution barred Houston from running again to succeed himself, the election of 1838 saw Vice President Mirabeau Lamar win the presidency. Despite serving in office—and in the revolution—together, Houston and Lamar were more rivals than colleagues. In the absence of formal political parties, Texas politics assumed an exceptionally personalized character, and Lamar had made himself the leader of the nascent anti-Houston faction. Yet Lamar's election should not necessarily be seen as an indication that the Texians were now rejecting Houston's leadership. There had been two candidates in the race with Houston's support, but both died prior to the election, leaving Lamar running essentially unopposed.[75]

While his election was largely by default, Lamar wasted no time in attempting to steer Texas onto a new course. In his inaugural address, Lamar made it clear that he would not pursue annexation, insisting that such an action "once taken would produce a lasting regret, and ultimately prove as disastrous to our liberty and hopes, as the triumphant sword of the enemy." For Lamar, annexation may have made sense in the aftermath of a revolution that devastated the country, but now, with independence and rich natural resources at its disposal, annexation had no benefits. Instead, Lamar unilaterally reoriented Texian foreign policy to focus on building Texas into a great power. He painted a vision of Texas as an expansive republic to rival the United States, "stretching from the Sabine to the Pacific and away to the South West as far as the obstinacy of the enemy may render it necessary for the sword to make the boundary."[76]

For all his dreams of empire, Lamar's administration soon stumbled. Despite concluding the treaty with France that Houston had initiated, Lamar failed to gain official recognition from Britain.[77] Similarly, he was unable to make any headway in convincing Mexico to recognize Texian independence, leaving the specter of another invasion hanging over the young nation. The new president also initiated a costly war with the Cherokee, repudiating the peace that Houston had negotiated.[78]

Yet the most prominent and disastrous policy of the Lamar administration was his attempt to assert Texian power further west. After independence, Texas had claimed that the lands now constituting New Mexico—at the time a Mexican territory called Santa Fe de Nuevo México—for itself. Indeed, Texas' claims were quite expansive, with the Texas Congress insisting at different times that Texas included substantial portions of what is now New Mexico, Arizona, Utah, Nevada, California, part of western Colorado, and the Mexican states of Baja California, Sonora, and northern Coahuila.[79] Although Texas did not have the strength to assert these claims, no less an authority than Andrew Jackson was purported to have advised the Texians that if they could "claim the Californias on the Pacific" that it would ease Texas' road to annexation by "paralyz[ing] the opposition of the North and East."[80] For his part, Lamar saw these claims as central to his goal of building Texas into a regional power. Unfortunately for the president, his initial proposal in 1839 to send an expeditionary force to conquer Santa Fe was rejected by Congress. Two years later, Lamar decided to circumvent Congress. Violating the Texas constitution, which held that only Congress could declare war and appropriate funds, Lamar appropriated $89,000 from the treasury and dispatched soldiers to seize Santa Fe. The result was a disaster. The expedition became lost and ran out of supplies, eventually surrendering to Mexican authorities and "hand[ing] Mexico a victory for which that country did not have to fire a single shot."[81] As summarized by Kenneth Hendrickson, Lamar "had come into office hoping to improve upon the administrative record of Sam Houston; instead, he had fared worse in almost every area."[82]

The disasters of the Lamar administration only made it easier for Houston to make his political comeback. After spending a year out of office, Houston ran for and won a seat in the Texas House of Representatives, remarking that he "might have been happy in ignorance at home had I known the full extent of Lamar's stupidity."[83] Once in Congress, Houston and his partisans dominated its proceedings.[84] He also remained in correspondence with Henderson and kept up to date on diplomatic issues "as if he had never stepped down from the presidential chair."[85] Staying involved and visible on the national scene, it was no surprise that Houston was once again a candidate for the presidency in 1841 and handily won election to a second non-consecutive term with nearly 75 percent of the vote.[86] Reassuming the presidential chair in December 1841, Houston informed the Texas Congress that the first item on his foreign policy agenda was to firmly define Texas' relationship with the United States, whether it be annexation or independence.[87]

CHAPTER 4

The Annexation Treaty

With Houston once again serving as president of Texas, and Tyler firmly set as president of the United States, the two men most responsible for bringing Texas into the Union were now in place at the heads of their respective executive branches. Yet their institutional and political circumstances could not be more different.

The accidental president Tyler was unelected and faced a strong two-party system where both parties found him repugnant. Democrats mistrusted him for abandoning their party and censuring Jackson during the bank removal controversy; Whigs considered him an apostate who had ridden their party to power and then single-handedly destroyed the Whig agenda. This animosity was so prevalent that one Whig congressman introduced articles of impeachment against Tyler. While the impeachment failed to go anywhere in the House, the effort made Tyler the first president to have impeachment articles drawn up against him.[1]

By contrast, Houston—still considered a hero of the Texas Revolution—had just been overwhelmingly reelected to a second non-consecutive term as soon as he was constitutionally eligible. Moreover, the lack of a party system in Texas meant there was no organized political opposition to Houston. As Stanley Siegel put it, Texas politics "were almost wholly of a personal nature" during the Republican period, and no person had greater sway within Texas than Sam Houston.[2] These different institutional and political positions would have a dramatic effect on how Tyler and Houston worked to bring about Texas annexation, particularly in the initial efforts to negotiate and ratify an annexation treaty.

For Houston, annexation was essential to his administration, and indeed, to the survival of Texas. Despite surviving long enough to have a peaceful transfer of power between two different presidential administrations, Texas' independence was not secure. Mexico had not recognized Texas as a sovereign nation, and the possibility that Mexico would mount a military campaign of reconquest to forcibly reintegrate the Lone Star Republic remained an ever-present danger.

In March 1842, it appeared this threat had become a reality as four hundred Mexican soldiers under the command of Colonel Rafael Vasquez conducted incursions into Texas. While Vasquez's force retired back to Mexico after two days, their brief foray saw them capture San Antonio, and it was only their voluntary withdrawal that returned San Antonio to Texian hands. Two other raids by Mexican troops seized the towns of Goliad and Refugio before similarly returning to Mexico after a few days. The raids revealed Texas' vulnerability and was interpreted by the Texians as a prelude to a full Mexican invasion.[3] In response, Houston issued a general call to arms as part of an "immediate preparation for defensive war."[4] His insistence on a defensive war was driven primarily by his assessment of Texas' relative military and economic strength. With the Texas economy in shambles and no organized Texas force ready to be deployed, Texas did not have the military or financial capabilities to retaliate against Mexico. The grim realities of being a young frontier republic had become frustratingly clear and severely limited Houston's options. In his message to Congress in June 1842, he explicitly declined to recommend that Congress pass a declaration of war and instead argued for enhancing the nation's border defenses.[5]

Despite Houston's reluctance, the mood of the people and Congress was to aggressively respond, with some pushing for an offensive invasion of Mexico.[6] In mid-July, the Texas Congress passed a declaration of war on Mexico. Along with declaring war, the legislation empowered the president to take personal command of the army and granted him "virtually dictatorial powers" to conscript soldiers and sell ten million acres of land. In Stanley Siegel's words, "if Houston desired to be a military strong man and to pose as the savior of the Republic, the opportunity was now at hand."[7]

The president, however, declined these powers, exercising his own constitutional authority to veto the measure. To Houston, the bill was not only inadvisable on a policy level, but also unconstitutional. In terms of policy, the same pressures that had convinced Houston to advocate for defensive measures remained. From his institutional position as president and experience as a military commander, he could clearly see that Texas was not prepared for the effort required to successfully invade Mexico. Logistically, it would require at least five thousand men—over five times larger than the army he had commanded at San Jacinto[8]—who would need to receive substantial training before the invasion could even start. Financially, Texas could not afford to field such a force. The provisions allowing the president to sell ten million acres of land were deemed by Houston to be "impracticable," as well as at odds with another provision that promised 640 acres to every volunteer or drafted militia man. Constitutionally, Houston doubted that Congress had the power to draft soldiers and send them "beyond our limits in a war of invasion," much less "to invest and clothe the Executive with extraordinary powers and discretion." Finally, Houston noted that if Texas proceeded to prosecute an offensive war in this fashion, personally led by a president imbued with dictatorial authority, it would set a precedent that would lead to "the destruction of the liberties of his country." The proper course, in Houston's mind, remained the enactment of defensive measures on the frontiers to prevent a Mexican invasion.[9]

Stymied by Houston's veto, Congress adjourned with Texas' national security still very much under threat. In September 1842, another Mexican force, this time commanded by General Adrian Woll, invaded Texas and once again captured San Antonio. After a week of occupying the city, a group of Texians organized themselves and managed to repel Woll's forces. This second incursion, while not the full-blown invasion that many expected, once again highlighted Texas' vulnerability. It also forced Houston's hand as he ordered a force of Texians down to the Rio Grande and authorized their commander, General Alexander Somervell, to proceed into Mexico "if you can advance with the prospect of success."[10] The resulting campaign was initially successful, but quickly degenerated into a disaster as a contingent of Somervell's soldiers mutinied when he refused to cross into Mexico. Appointing their own commander, the mutineers entered Mexican territory and occupied the town of Mier, where they were engaged and forced to surrender by Mexican soldiers. Taken prisoner, they were marched through the barren mountains of northern Mexico with little food or water before arriving at a hacienda where one-tenth of the Texian force was executed.[11] Thus, by the end of 1842, Texas' military situation was dire, having been subject to raids, economically unable to mount a determined response, and with Texian soldiers executed by Mexican forces and others held as veritable prisoners of war.

Recognizing Texas' military shortcomings, Houston turned to diplomacy to preserve the Lone Star Republic without engaging in another war with Mexico. Above all, his primary foreign policy goal remained annexation, and he appointed men to his administration who shared his vision of bringing Texas into the Union. The most notable of these subordinates was Secretary of State Anson Jones. Jones had served as the Texian minister to the United States during Houston's first term and been a loyal supporter of the Raven in the 1841 campaign. Such service convinced Houston that despite Jones' clear presidential ambitions, he could be relied on as a staunch proponent of annexation.[12] Rounding out Houston's chief diplomatic lieutenants were James Reily as chargé d'affaires to the United States and Ashbel Smith as chargé d'affaires to Britain and France.[13]

Yet even with the expansionist Tyler in the White House, Houston's initial attempts to initiate annexation negotiations in 1842 were rebuffed. Tyler himself remained in favor of annexation, as it fit perfectly with both his general ideological bent towards American expansion and his need for a landmark political victory. But the volatile political situation in Washington made him cautious. The Whigs held both houses of Congress and were eager to punish the partyless president as much as possible.

In addition to Tyler's personal unpopularity, annexation itself was liable to inflame sectional tensions, and American annexationists did little to sooth those fears. In an attempt to see some movement on the issue, in January 1842, Representative Henry Wise of Virginia made a purely sectional speech arguing that Texas was necessary for the South to maintain political equilibrium with the North. A few months later, Wise accused Britain of seeking to control Texas in order to abolish slavery and ultimately dissolve the Union, while also framing the ongoing conflict between Texas and Mexico as a battle between pro- and anti-slavery forces. These extravagant arguments were seized upon by opponents of annexation, particularly Northern abolitionists and their congressional allies. Chief among them was John Quincy Adams, who framed the entire issue as part of a "slave-breeding conspiracy against the freedom of the north."[14] Other annexationists, such as Virginia Representative Thomas Walker Gilmer, attempted to be more measured and emphasize the national benefits of annexation. Gilmer foreshadowed arguments Tyler himself would make for annexation by stressing the economic possibilities for both free and slave states that would accompany Texas into the Union.

The sectional divide even infiltrated Tyler's administration. Despite insisting "that the great interests of the north would be incalculably advanced by such an acquisition," Tyler was unable to convince Secretary of State Daniel Webster to support annexation.[15] While Webster upheld the American line that Texas was a recognized sovereign nation—even defending the young republic against Mexican claims to the contrary[16]— the former Massachusetts senator was attuned to the antislavery sentiment in New England and concerned enough about his political future to know that he could not embrace annexation.[17] In addition to Webster, the American minister to Great Britain, Edward Everett, was another New Englander who was "so disgusted" by the prospect that Texas annexation could expand slavery that "he thought of resigning" once it started to become a major issue.[18]

The fact that two Northerners could hold such high offices in the State Department and essentially veto a potential annexation policy concerned the southerners in Tyler's cabinet, particularly Secretary of the Navy Abel Upshur. Upshur was a native Virginian and lifelong friend of Tyler as well as a well-known advocate of strict construction and states' rights.[19] Seeing his old friend put aside his expansionist dreams, Upshur worried that the president had abandoned both his principles and the South by retaining the two New Englanders and deferring to them on foreign policy measures. In a letter lamenting Everett's position in London, Upshur bemoaned that "the present condition of the country imperiously requires that a Southern man and a slave holder should represent us at [the British] court . . . And yet a Boston man is appointed, half school-master, half priest, & whole abolitionist!" The only way the secretary could make sense of it was by viewing Tyler as making a "concession to Webster." Yet such a concession, in Uphsur's view, struck at the heart of Tyler's natural constituency and political base, remarking that "if Tyler has any party at all, it is that party [the Southern states' rightists] which he treats on all occasions with utter neglect."[20]

These sectional tensions and policy disagreements within his own cabinet, combined with congressional opposition and his own lack of popular support, convinced the president that he could not yet press forward on annexation. As relayed by Reily,

> annexation was spoken of by the *few* warm and ardent friends of the measure, including the President . . . yet at no time was it discussed as a probable event. All parties were satisfied that no treaty of annexation would be ratified by the Senate, and there was not even a majority in favor of the policy in the lower House.[21]

Because of this political dynamic, when Houston offered to open negotiations concerning annexation on two separate occasions in 1842, he was turned down both times. Yet it was not simply a lack of political will or a sycophantic deference to Webster that stopped Tyler from engaging with Houston. Tyler was also trying to protect some of his other policy initiatives and believed that to open the debate on annexation could threaten gains in other areas. Specifically, Houston's annexation offers were made while the Tyler administration was attempting to negotiate and ratify what became the Webster-Ashburton Treaty with the British, which concerned numerous border disputes that had been left unresolved by prior treaties. At the same time, another boundary dispute with Britain over the Oregon Territory was ongoing, and Tyler hoped to resolve that issue as well, firmly setting the entire northern boundary of the United States with British Canada. Engaging in discussion over Texas, with ramifications for the future of slavery, would not only require the administration's full attention, but could doom the president's larger diplomatic efforts.[22] In short, Tyler's comprehensive view of his administration's political shortcomings, internal division, and diplomatic agenda forced him to prioritize his goals. In doing so, he recognized that Texas, the biggest prize he could pursue, had to be left for later.

Tyler's decision to defer on Texas continued into the early months of 1843, when Reily was replaced as chargé d'affaires to Washington by another Houston lieutenant, Isaac Van Zandt. In his meetings with Van Zandt, Tyler reiterated his support for annexation, but once again insisted that the time was not right. In a letter reporting on the situation, Van Zandt commented that Tyler had assured him that "the moment he considered it safe to do so he would advise me of the desire of his Govt to enter into the negotiation." In Van Zandt's view, the two major obstacles were the Senate's opposition and Webster's position as secretary of state. Regarding the former, the Senate had "much embarrassed" the president by rejecting several major cabinet appointments, signaling that it would not welcome any of the president's measures, particularly something as controversial as annexation. As to the latter, Van Zandt believed that without Webster in the State Department, "a better opportunity will be afforded for operation."[23] But until those obstacles were removed, annexation was a non-starter in Washington.

The European Option

With Tyler dragging his feet, Houston turned most of his diplomatic attention to Britain and France. Both nations had substantial interests in preventing Texas from joining the United States.[24] French Foreign Minister François Guizot believed that annexation would lead to the full American conquest of Mexico, disrupting France's own relations with that country. Moreover, Guizot thought that France's own prestige would suffer because it had been the first European nation to recognize Texas as a sovereign nation.[25] The British similarly sought to prevent the expansion of American power and hoped Texas would act "as a barrier to the United States on their S. Western frontier" and be "a market and rival producer of cotton . . . to the United States."[26] From Britain's perspective, Texas could serve as a political and commercial counterweight to the United States, creating a balance of power in North America and providing British industry with another source of raw goods as well as the opportunity to wean itself from its dependence on American commodities, particularly cotton.²⁷ Given Texas' vulnerable position, some in the British government also hoped it could pressure the Texians "to abandon slave labor in exchange for the support necessary to ensure the long-term success of their Republic."²⁸

Given the options between a standoffish United States and moderately receptive European powers, it is no surprise that Houston made a considerable effort to improve Texas' relations with Britain and France. In the short term, an alliance with these great powers could help secure Texas from further Mexican incursions, as foreign pressure might finally lead Mexico to officially recognize Texas' independence. But even beyond protecting Texian sovereignty, Houston believed he could leverage British and French support for an independent Texas in a way that served his primary goal of annexation. Specifically, Houston hoped to provoke Tyler and the Americans into acting on annexation by cozying up to the Europeans.²⁹ Developing closer relationships with the Europeans would give the impression that if Texas persisted as an independent nation, it could very well find itself in a European power's sphere of influence. Such a state of affairs would be intolerable for the Americans on three levels. First, having a close ally of Britain or France—or both—on its southwestern border posed a significant risk to national security. Second, expansionists in the United States would immediately recognize that a European-backed Texas might block further efforts at western expansion. Perhaps even more concerning, Texas could become a rival in westward expansion and potentially grow into a major power in its own right, just as Mirabeau Lamar had hoped. Third, American slaveholders viewed European—and particularly British—influence as a threat to the peculiar institution. If British abolitionists gained a foothold in Texas, or even convinced the Lone Star Republic to abolish slavery, it would have major negative ramifications for the South and the continued existence of American slavery. While Houston hoped that all this might be enough to convince the Americans to act, in the event that they did not, alliances with Britain and France could still serve their secondary purpose of fortifying Texas' independence and bolstering its future security.

As France had already formally recognized Texas, negotiations with Britain initially focused on receiving diplomatic recognition. Some of the work to achieve British recognition of Texas had been done prior to Houston's second term, but it was not until June 1842 that the treaties were finally signed and Texas was formally recognized by the British government.[30] Britain also agreed to serve as a mediator between Texas and Mexico in an effort to create a lasting peace. The Texians hoped such a promise was the beginning of a larger joint effort between Britain, France, and the United States to pressure Mexico into recognizing Texas' independence. In this, however, the Houston administration was less successful. Mexico repeatedly refused offers of mediation from both Britain and the United States. Ultimately, the British and French governments determined that "a Joint mediation of Great Britain, France, and the United States for the purpose of effecting an accommodation between Mexico and Texas would not under present circumstances answer any good purpose" and instead suggested "it would be better on all accounts that each party should act separately, but similarly."[31]

The breakdown of tripartite mediation left Houston in an exposed position at the beginning of 1843. Mexico remained committed to reunification, and the Tyler administration was still unwilling to pursue annexation. Of his limited options, working with Britain appeared to be the best alternative, both to deter Mexican aggression as well as to continue prompting the United States into action on the theory that the Americans would be unable to tolerate a British-aligned Texas. Essentially, Houston hoped to pit the two greatest English-speaking powers in the world against each other and in doing so place Texas in a win-win situation. As summarized by Freehling,

> If he [Houston] could rouse specters of British re-entry into the Western Hemisphere, British-hating Americans might rouse John Tyler from his timidity. A more decisive Tyler effort to annex Texas might alarm Englishmen into protection of an independent Texas. The expanded English push might yield a more committed American pull, then a greater English shove, and so on. Now that circle was not vicious at all for a Texas patriot trying to counter America's failure to act.[32]

Houston personally took charge of enticing Britain to bring Texas into its sphere of influence. He informed Charles Elliot, the British chargé d'affaires and consul general in Texas, that he "desire[d] to see Texas occupy an independent position among the Nation's [sic] of the earth" and suggested that if "the independence of Texas should be recognized through the medium of English influence," then annexation to the United States might never take place.[33]

This potential alliance seemed to bear some fruit in the spring of 1843 when Santa Anna, reinstated as ruler of Mexico, offered Houston a peace proposal. Under this proposal, Texas would once again become part of Mexico, but those involved in the prior rebellion would be granted amnesty, no Mexican troops would be stationed in Texas, and Texas would have autonomy over its internal affairs. While this was clearly unacceptable to Houston, the British supported it, and Houston made a show about seriously entertaining the idea. He sent commissioners to Mexico City to negotiate with Santa Anna and even declared an armistice with Mexico on June 13, 1843.[34] Such actions were part of Houston's strategy of playing the bigger powers off each other. With Britain supporting peace talks with Mexico, the negotiations suggested that Houston's situation was desperate enough for reintegration into Mexico to be a serious possibility, one which would not go unnoticed by annexationists in the United States.

Yet even as Houston and his administration worked to leverage Britain to achieve their own policy priorities, the cost of British support was higher than many Texian slaveholders were willing to pay. From his diplomatic post in London, Ashbel Smith repeatedly highlighted that although the British supported Texas' continuing existence, slavery remained a major stumbling block for Anglo-Texian relations. This was no surprise to the Texians. One of the three treaties that accompanied British recognition of Texas had been a treaty committing Texas to the suppression of the African slave trade, and Elliot was a noted abolitionist.[35] Smith, however, believed that further guarantees of British support for Texian independence—including future mediation with Mexico and trade privileges—could depend on whether Texas abolished slavery.[36] British Foreign Secretary Lord Aberdeen even confirmed in a meeting with Smith in July 1843 that Britain had an interest in Texas abolition as part of its larger interest in international abolitionism and commitment "to abolish slavery every where."[37] In Smith's view, the British position was not altogether altruistic, but had the geopolitical aim of isolating the United States as a slaveholding power. If Texas became a free republic supported by the British, Smith contended that it would inexorably lead to the "death [of] the slave holding states of the American Union," as they would be "hemmed in between the free states on their northern border, and a free Anglo Saxon State on their southern border."[38] Despite Aberdeen's insistence that the British government had no intention to "interfere improperly" with Texas' internal institutions, Smith remained suspicious, and suggested any attempts to impose abolition would be "derogatory to our national honor."[39] That Smith and the Texians would have such a response to even the suggestion of abolitionism illustrates their commitment to retaining slavery.

While these were serious concerns for the Texians, the Houston administration nonetheless found a way to fold them into the president's broader strategy of trying to spur American action. Specifically, the Texians made sure that Britain's abolitionist overtures were brought to the Americans' attention. Writing from London, Smith warned the American proslavery extremist John C. Calhoun that the British sought to abolish slavery in Texas "as an entering wedge to the abolition of slavery in the United States."[40] He also urged Van Zandt, his counterpart in Washington, to tell friendly proslavery members of Congress about Britain's abolitionist machinations, and, if possible, to tell Tyler himself.[41] Van Zandt happily obliged this request. Meeting with the American president and "one of the prominent members of his cabinet" (most likely Upshur), the Texian diplomat shared Smith's correspondence and added the claim that Mexico's "prime reason" for seeking to reconquer Texas was to abolish slavery.[42] Such information—and the threat it posed to Southern slavery—had a significant effect on the annexationists within the administration, including the president. As we shall see, "Houston's and Jones's ruse of scaring the United States was entirely successful."[43]

Tyler Changes Course

The news from Texas, along with the conclusion of the Webster-Ashburton Treaty and other diplomatic endeavors, convinced Tyler that his administration had gone as far as it could with Webster as secretary of state, and the president began pressuring the New Englander to resign. Seeing that Tyler no longer valued his advice and was determined to pursue annexation, Webster took the hint and resigned in the spring of 1843. In his place, Tyler appointed his old friend Upshur.[44] Upshur's appointment was welcome news to annexationists in Texas, with Van Zandt declaring him "one of the best appointments that could be made for the interests of Texas . . . devoted in his attachment to our country, and anxious to promote our cause."[45] Tyler also sent Duff Green, a Southerner with close ties to Calhoun and Upshur, as an unofficial representative to Europe.[46] With Upshur in the State Department and Green as a source in Britain and France, Tyler now had an administration staffed by committed annexationists.

Uphsur's initial actions regarding Texas illustrate how effective Houston's diplomacy with the British had been in provoking American action. The prospect of Texas not only moving into the British orbit but also abolishing slavery deeply troubled the Southern diplomat. Writing to Calhoun in August 1843, Upshur insisted that the South must immediately push for Texas' annexation as a slave state. To leave Texas independent, or even to admit Texas as a free state, would "be fatal to the Union, & ruinous to the whole country." Moreover, Upshur saw the issue as clearly "a *Southern* question" on which the South must unite "as one man" rather than remaining divided into parties.[47] Seeing annexation as a purely sectional issue, Upshur worked to determine if the British had made any headway in convincing the Texians to abolish slavery.

At the same, Lord Aberdeen unwittingly poured fuel on the fire of the southerner's paranoid suspicions. During a debate in the House of Lords, an antislavery member asked the foreign secretary what he was doing about Texas. After stating that Britain was mediating peace talks between Texas and Mexico, he casually added that "no one was more anxious than himself to see the abolition of slavery in Texas," a statement Aberdeen's interlocutor declared would be "received with joy by all who were favorable to the object of the Anti-Slavery Societies."[48] While the exchange only reiterated Aberdeen's—and the British government's—general position of opposing slavery generally, suspicious and Anglophobic Americans saw it as evidence of a broader conspiracy against slavery in the United States. Suspecting Aberdeen was implying a broader effort to force abolition in the United States, Upshur rushed to instruct Everett to investigate the intentions of the British government, and specifically if it was actively seeking to abolish slavery in Texas. If it was, Upshur made clear that he viewed such efforts as a direct attack on slavery in the United States, constituting an undue interference into American affairs by a foreign power. More broadly, Upshur viewed this as a question of great power politics, and a way for Britain to threaten America's economic interests. Coming to the same conclusion that Smith had, Upshur remarked that Britain's pursuit of abolition was not due to "a mere feeling of philanthropy," but rather was intended "to destroy, as far as possible, the rivalry and competition . . . of the United States."[49]

More importantly for Upshur and the Texians, Aberdeen's comments convinced Tyler that the time had finally come to act on his long-held dream of Texas annexation. In September 1843, Tyler informed Upshur of his decision to pursue annexation "in the form of a treaty, and authorized him at once, and without delay, to communicate that fact to Mr. Van Zandt."[50] Upshur excitedly did exactly that, reaching out to Van Zandt to open secret negotiations.[51]

Surprisingly, it was now the Texians' turn to be reluctant to pursue annexation. As part of opening talks with Mexico the previous summer, the Houston administration had instructed Van Zandt to no longer pursue annexation talks.[52] When Van Zandt wrote to his superiors about Upshur's offer, Houston demurred. Given the military threat posed by Mexico, Houston calculated that it was better to continue negotiations with Mexico and attempt to secure a peace than to begin negotiations with the United States over an abstract threat to slavery.[53] Houston went so far as to declare that he did not think the British were a threat to Texian slavery, remarking in a speech "that England does not *care* about the abolition of slavery."[54] More seriously, the president discussed Upshur's offer with Elliot and once again assured the British chargé d'affaires that if Mexico recognized Texas' independence, he would not pursue annexation to the United States.

That Houston would make what appeared to be a sudden about face is not completely surprising given his situation. As related to Van Zandt by Jones, Houston had not "change[d] in his views of the general policy" of annexation but was only responding to "a change in the relations of this country [Texas] with other powers," specifically, the British-mediated negotiations with Mexico. Having entered into talks with Mexico, Houston was close to achieving diplomatic recognition and removing the constant threat of Mexican invasion, as well as securing the superpower British Empire as an ally. Yet if he moved towards annexation now, he might provoke Mexico into an attack and sour relations with Britain. Moreover, Houston and Jones were well aware that despite Tyler's renewed enthusiasm, the Virginian's relationship with the Senate had not improved. While the Whigs had lost the House in the 1842 midterm elections, they still controlled the Senate and remained solidly opposed to Tyler's administration. Thus, even if a treaty could be made, its ratification in the American Senate remained "of very uncertain attainment." In short, if Texas pursued an annexation treaty and it failed, the young republic would be "in a much worse situation than she is at present... without a friend and her difficulties with Mexico unsettled."[55]

Houston also likely knew that Tyler would not lose interest in Texas and could afford to make his American counterpart wait and feel some of the consternation and anxiety he had experienced for his entire presidency. With Britain cultivating an alliance with Texas and Mexico open to recognition, annexation was not a pressing necessity for Texian national security. Summarizing the change in Texas' diplomatic situation between 1842 and 1843, Houston declared in a speech that where Texas had previously "encountered nothing but indifference, apathy, coldness and neglect" from the United States, Britain, and France, now "each of the nations is striving to rival and outstrip the others in conferring benefits upon us."[56] For the first time, Texas had real options and the potential to craft its own Manifest Destiny.

Tyler and Upshur, however, were not willing to let their collective vision of an annexed Texas die. While Tyler did not address annexation as a policy goal in his annual message to Congress—an omission which surprised many observers and dismayed annexation advocates—the administration diligently lobbied senators to support a potential annexation treaty. As part of this effort, Tyler also had Upshur press the

United States' claims in the Oregon Territory in the hope that the prospect of resolving the Oregon question might make Texas more palatable to Northern senators and emphasize the national scope of his endeavors.[57] In January 1844, Tyler and Upshur were convinced that they had the numbers, and Upshur reached out to both Van Zandt and the American chargé d'affaires in Texas, William Sumter Murphy, informing them that he was certain two-thirds of the Senate would ratify an annexation treaty if it was presented. Notably, Upshur also made informal and unwritten promises to Van Zandt, reassuring the Texian that as soon as the treaty was signed Tyler would deploy military forces to protect Texas from any Mexican retaliation.[58] Murphy, acting without instructions from Upshur, made similar reassurances to Houston, but did so in writing and suggested the support would come prior to signing the treaty.[59]

The administration's lobbying gained further aid from outside sources. Senator Robert J. Walker of Mississippi published a pamphlet making the case for the national benefits of annexation. Walker even went so far as to argue that abolitionists should support annexation because it could create a "safety valve" through which slaves might escape to freedom in Mexico, a variation of the diffusion theory Tyler had supported during the debate over the Missouri Compromise.[60] More significantly, former president Jackson weighed in to voice his support, warning that if the United States did not bring Texas into the Union now, then it would fall into the British sphere of influence and allow Britain to cut off American expansion westward, as well as strengthen British claims to the Oregon Territory.[61] He also wrote to Houston to encourage his former protégé to open negotiations and impress upon him the necessity of annexation.[62]

In his reply, Houston noted his "duty, as Executive, to have an eye to every emergency which might possibly arise" but assured his old commander that he was "determined upon immediate annexation to the United States." While he contended that the United States had more to gain from annexation than Texas—remarking that "Texas with peace could exist without the U. States; but the U. States cannot . . . exist without Texas"—he nonetheless agreed that now was the time for Texas to join the Union.[63] Seeing the time as right, the president recommended the Texas Congress take *"immediate action"* in sending another envoy to Washington to help with negotiations.[64]

When Van Zandt finally began talks with Upshur over what a treaty might look like, both presidents made sure to keep the negotiations secret. Houston did not end his discussions with Mexico and continued to work with the British as he had before.[65] Tyler similarly declined to make any sort of public statement and did not inform Congress that there was major movement towards annexation.[66] For their part, Van Zandt and Upshur worked quickly, finishing a draft of the treaty on February 27, 1844.

That momentum, however, would soon come to a screeching halt. The day after finishing the treaty, Tyler, Upshur, and members of Congress and the administration went for a demonstration cruise on the Potomac River aboard the new warship, the *U.S.S. Princeton*. The main part of the display was the firing of one of the ship's largest guns, the ironically named "Peacemaker." After firing several rounds, the attendees went below deck to enjoy refreshments. When Upshur and others returned to the deck—the president notably stayed below—the captain of the *Princeton* was urged to fire "Peacemaker" again. This time, however, the gun exploded, killing six and wounding several others. Among the dead was Secretary of State Upshur.[67]

The New Secretary of State

Upshur's untimely death left annexation in doubt. Writing to Jones, Van Zandt lamented that had he received instructions from the Texas government earlier "the treaty could have been concluded in half a day," and he feared that the next American secretary of state might not be so capable in pushing annexation through.[68] For his part, Tyler was unsure how to proceed. Annexation was at a critical point, and he needed a secretary who not only supported the policy but would be able to shepherd it through a hostile Senate. For Tyler's pro-annexation friends, however, the choice was clear: Upshur's mentor and friend John C. Calhoun.[69]

By 1844, Calhoun had firmly established himself as the political and ideological leader of the South. A former vice president to both Adams and Jackson, Calhoun had spent most of the previous decade as a senator from South Carolina, articulating a vision of states' rights where the states could nullify acts of the national government and arguing that slavery was a "positive good."[70] While Tyler was also a staunch supporter of states' rights and a slaveowner, he did not go as far as Calhoun did, opposing nullification and holding to the traditional Jeffersonian view that slavery was an evil which should eventually be abolished.[71] Calhoun's close identification with the South meant that if he was made secretary of state and placed in charge of the annexation treaty, it would immediately become a sectional issue despite Tyler's consistent efforts to frame it as in the national interest, benefitting North and South. As summarized by Norma Peterson, "Calhoun tended to emphasize the sectional and slavery aspect; Tyler tried to minimize it, while stressing the economic and strategic values."[72] Tyler himself later reflected that Calhoun had consistently "narrowed down the [Texas] question to the comparatively contemptible ground of Southern and local interest" against his wishes.[73] Notably, Tyler also objected to Calhoun's sectionalism on the grounds that it was at odds with the nature of the presidency itself, commenting that Calhoun had attempted to "substantially convert the executive into a mere Southern agency in place of being what it truly was—the representative of American interests, whether those interests were North, South, East, or West."[74]

The reasons for why Tyler ultimately chose Calhoun to replace Upshur are not altogether clear and the sources are contradictory. Virginia congressman Henry Wise claimed that he spoke with Calhoun's friends about the position without clearing it with Tyler, giving Calhoun the impression that the offer came directly from the president and putting Tyler in a position where he could not then rescind the offer without potentially losing Southern support. Other sources claim that Tyler had repeatedly sought to appoint Calhoun to the State Department and it was only now that the South Carolinian accepted.[75] Dan Monroe has speculated that Tyler's recruitment of Calhoun was bound up in his electoral ambitions. As Calhoun had already withdrawn from the 1844 presidential race, Tyler might have predicted that with Calhoun in the cabinet the former vice president would back the sitting president in the coming election, allowing Tyler to co-opt Calhoun's significant political base.[76] Whatever the ultimate reason, whether he felt bound to honor an offer he did not make or whether he really wanted to bring Calhoun into the cabinet for an electoral advantage, Tyler nominated and the Senate confirmed Calhoun as secretary of state.[77] In his letter informing Calhoun of the appointment, the president made it clear that the first of the "great ends to be accomplished" would be concluding annexation.[78]

Despite appointing Calhoun, Tyler recognized that his new secretary's involvement would inextricably link annexation with a defense of slavery, and as Calhoun was not in Washington at the time of his confirmation, Tyler rushed to try and conclude the treaty himself before Calhoun returned to take up his duties. The president met directly with Van Zandt to try and finish the details, but the Texian could not conclude the treaty, as he was waiting for the arrival of James P. Henderson—a former Texas secretary of state—whom Houston had sent to assist with negotiations. By the time Henderson finally arrived in Washington, so had Calhoun, with the latter taking up his duties on April 1, 1844.[79]

As the president and his new secretary of state met with the Texians, it became evident that Houston was still concerned about Mexican retaliation and sought additional guarantees of military protection.[80] Upshur's prior verbal commitments were no longer enough, the Texians now wanted these guarantees in writing. Tyler obliged and with those assurances the treaty was finally signed by Calhoun, Van Zandt, and Henderson on April 12, 1844.[81]

The terms of the treaty would have allowed Texas to enter the United States as a territory, with the national government assuming all the debts accrued by the Republic of Texas during its independence up to $10 million, with the sale of Texas' public lands set to help pay off that debt. All Texas officials would retain their positions in the government, with the exception of the president, vice president, and members of the Texas cabinet. The treaty also outlined issues concerning property and real estate during the transfer of sovereignty. Finally, both sides had six months to have the treaty ratified by their respective senates.[82]

Back in Texas, Houston was happy with the provisions of the treaty, telling Jones, "It had as well been made in Texas."[83] He believed the provisions making Texas into a territory were constitutionally correct, even remarking that he "would be extremely sorry" if the actions which brought Texas into the Union violated the Constitution for the sake of "*expediency*." At the same time, the president voiced his frustration that the military guarantees provided by Calhoun did not go as far as he had thought they would. He had taken a gamble by choosing to pursue annexation while still in negotiations with Mexico, and if it now failed—a failure Houston asserted would fall solely on "a want of action on the part of the U.S."—then Texas would be "without any security against the consequences which may result." Of course, if annexation did fail, he had already laid the groundwork for a backup plan by working with the British and the French, and Houston insisted the administration would simply "redouble our energies" to assure Texas became "sovereign and independent, founded upon her incalculable advantages of situation, and sustained by European influences without the slightest compromittal [sic] to her nationality." Reflecting the irritation of a man whose annexation dreams had been repeatedly dashed for the past decade, the president told Van Zandt and Henderson that this would be "the last effort at Annexation that Texas will ever make, nor do I believe that any solicitation or guarantee from the U.S. would at any future day induce her to consent to the measure."[84] The future of the young republic was at a crossroads, but the decision on which path it would take would not be decided in Austin, but over 1,500 miles away in Washington, D.C.

The Senate Weighs In

From the day it was signed, it took ten days for the treaty to be delivered to the American Senate. While there were a variety of reasons for why the Tyler administration took so long, the primary cause for delay was a letter from Richard Pakenham, the British ambassador to the United States.[85] Pakenham had forwarded a dispatch from Lord Aberdeen to Upshur prior to the latter's death where Aberdeen insisted that despite the British government's general opposition to slavery it had no specific designs on abolishing slavery in Texas. Calhoun found this letter in Upshur's files and wrote a lengthy reply soon after signing the treaty.

In his reply, Calhoun maintained that he had been "directed by the President" to respond to Aberdeen, particularly to the claim that Britain sought abolish slavery "throughout the world." Calhoun interpreted this claim as a threat and, informing Pakenham of the recently signed treaty, framed American annexation of Texas as a form of self-defense, asserting that if Britain gained a foothold in an independent Texas it would endanger "the prosperity and safety of this union." Such an argument aligned with Tyler's prior arguments about annexation producing national benefits for the country as whole. Yet Calhoun did not stop there. The second half of the letter saw Calhoun pivot into a positive argument for slavery, contending that annexation was for the benefit of slavery, and by extension, of the South.[86]

Despite Calhoun's insistence that he had been directed by Tyler to write the letter, it is unclear how much Tyler agreed with the substance of Calhoun's reply. Reflecting on annexation in 1850, Tyler insisted that his personal view of the issue had not been "narrow and bigoted" but "embraced the whole country and all its interests."[87] His message to the Senate introducing the treaty reinforced this approach, focusing on the Texians' historic connections to the United States and the benefits each section would gain from admitting Texas.[88] In Tyler's telling, "Mr. Calhoun unceasingly talked of slavery and its abolition in connection with the subject. That idea seemed to possess him and Upshur *as a single idea*."[89] Yet, as Christopher Leahy notes, Tyler made no objections to the letter at the time, only doing so in retrospect, and it is certainly possible that Tyler allowed Calhoun to make the argument in an effort to simultaneously highlight the national and sectional cases for annexation, despite his own personal history of not embracing Calhoun's "positive good" argument for slavery.[90]

Whether or not Tyler knew of the letter, its inclusion with the treaty sent to the Senate undermined Tyler's efforts to present annexation in national rather than sectional terms. Jackson perceptively described this problem and condemned Calhoun for "display[ing] a great weakness and folly" through his decision to "introduce into matter that did not belong to the subject and well calculated to arouse the Eastern states against the annexation of Texas."[91] Representing the attitude of many northerners who implicitly connected annexation to slavery, Adams wrote in his diary that "the treaty for the annexation of Texas to this Union was this day sent to the Senate; and with it went the freedom of the human race."[92]

Sectionalism was not the only issue that proponents of annexation had to overcome. Mexico persisted in claiming that Texas remained a part of its union and warned the administration that any moves towards annexation would be viewed as an act of war.[93] Tyler had previously dismissed the threat posed by Mexico in his communications with Congress, telling them in December 1843 that such provocations could not cow "the representatives of a brave and patriotic people."[94] But by May 1844, the threat was serious enough that Tyler not only opened up negotiations with Mexico to facilitate their acceptance of the treaty, but also financed naval operations in the Gulf of Mexico to protect Texas from retaliation. Notably, the latter action was funded through the president's secret service funds, money which Congress provided to presidents to help with financing sensitive diplomatic missions. Tyler's use of these funds to support military actions on Texas' behalf was deemed to be unconstitutional by Tyler's treasury secretary, John Spencer, who refused to allocate the money. When Spencer remained obstinate in his refusal to act, Tyler removed him and ordered the action anyway.[95]

For many senators, however, the threat of a war with Mexico combined with domestic unrest between North and South overwhelmed any benefits that annexing Texas would bring. Remarkably, the most vehement opponent of the treaty was Senator Thomas Hart Benton, a Democrat from Missouri. Benton was a slaveholder and an ardent expansionist who considered himself "the oldest friend of Texas and the original annexation man."[96] Yet as a long-standing opponent of Calhoun, he reacted negatively to the South Carolinian's proslavery arguments, rejecting the notion that the treaty was a measure against British interference with slavery. Moreover, Benton was concerned that the treaty lacked a definitive border, highlighting that to annex Texas would also mean "annexing a boundary dispute two thousand miles in length."[97]

The questions raised by Benton about annexation inflaming sectional tensions and causing a war with Mexico were central to the treaty debate, which ran from May 16 to June 8. When the final vote was taken on June 8, the Senate rejected the treaty by an overwhelming vote of 35–16. Surprisingly, the vote did not break down neatly along sectional lines. Among the Whigs, all but one, John Henderson of Mississippi, voted against the treaty. The Democrats, by contrast, did split on the slavery question. Benton proved to be the only Southern Democrat to vote against the treaty, yet he was joined by a majority of Northern Democrats.[98]

The American Constitution requires treaties to be ratified by a two-thirds vote in order to ensure that whatever measures govern foreign policy are supported by a broad popular consensus. Yet here was a situation where a treaty had been rejected by two-thirds, clearly demonstrating a broad consensus against annexation. Tyler and Houston had gambled on the US Senate, and they had lost.

CHAPTER 5

The Elections of 1844

The Senate's rejection of the Texas treaty was a major blow to the annexation cause. Yet the timing proved to be fortuitous for the annexationists. With all the delay over negotiating the treaty, by the time it was signed and debated the 1844 presidential election in the United States was in full swing. Thus, even though the Senate had weighed in, the possibility remained for Tyler and Houston to ensure that annexation became the defining issue of the campaign.

Candidates, Parties, and Platforms

On April 27, 1844, the day that the treaty was sent to the Senate, the two frontrunners for the Whig and Democratic nominations, Clay and Van Buren, respectively, published letters in major newspapers opposing immediate annexation.[1] That both candidates felt the need to do this illustrates how central annexation had already become to national politics, with Adams even writing in his diary that Tyler had effectively "compelled" Clay and Van Buren "to stake their last chance upon opposition" to immediate annexation.[2]

Clay's nomination by the Whigs was a foregone conclusion. The leader of the party since its inception and the dominant figure in the Senate, no other Whig had the same level of clout within the party. While he had been passed over for the nomination in 1836 and 1840, Clay refused to cede the position of the Whigs' standard-bearer to someone else. He did not, however, want his candidacy to center on annexation.

In his letter, published in the *National Intelligencer*, Clay outlined his objections and condemned Tyler for "ventur[ing] upon so grave and momentous a proceeding, not only without any general manifestation of public opinion in favor of it, but in direct opposition to strong and decided expressions of public disapprobation." Despite admitting that he had not read the treaty yet, Clay elaborated on his opposition to immediate annexation. Acknowledging his previous actions as secretary of state working to bring Texas into the Union nearly twenty years earlier, Clay insisted that changed circumstances made annexation unacceptable. Specifically, he warned that "annexation and war with Mexico are identical," and Clay anticipated that Britain and France might very well join in such a conflict on Mexico's side.

Even if Mexico ceded Texas, Clay argued that domestic concerns would still compel him to oppose it. Clay particularly focused on the need to develop the western lands which made up the Louisiana Purchase before adding yet another vast territory. More seriously, there was the sectional issue, which Clay denounced on the grounds that trying to annex Texas for the purpose of strengthening the South would "sow the seeds of a dissolution of the Union." Furthermore, he did not think bringing Texas in would necessarily strengthen the South, speculating that the North might annex Canada in response or break Texas up into five smaller states, only two of which would likely be suited to the kind of agricultural production conducive to slavery as practiced elsewhere in the South. Yet after making these points, Clay concluded with language that obfuscated his intention, remarking that he considered annexation as dangerous to the Union "at this time." That qualifier left open the possibility that Clay might again change his mind about annexation despite the robust arguments he had just leveled against it.[3]

On the Democratic side, Van Buren had spent his time out of office preparing for his political comeback and he retained the hesitancy he had expressed about annexation as president. In his own public letter to the *Washington Daily Globe*, Van Buren focused on the substantive questions of whether it was constitutional and expedient to add Texas to the Union. To the first question, Van Buren argued that there was nothing unconstitutional about annexing Texas as a territory using the treaty process, it was only if the treaty attempted to bring in Texas as a full state that the process would, in his view, be unconstitutional.

On the second question, the former president had substantial reservations. Addressing his own past history with annexation—supporting it as secretary of state and then deciding against it as president—Van Buren did not find that enough had changed since his administration to convince him to change his mind. Like Clay, Van Buren worried that annexation would provoke Mexico into a war. But unlike Clay, Van Buren directly addressed the concern that Texas might become a pawn of European powers, or, more specifically, "a British colony or dependency." The former president considered such an outcome highly unlikely and not something to be overly worried about. He did, however, admit that "if the time ever comes when the question resolves itself into whether Texas shall become a British dependency or colony, or a constitutional portion of this Union, the great principle of self-defence [sic] . . . would, without doubt, produce as great a unanimity among us in favor of the latter alternative, as can ever be expected."[4] Yet for the present, Van Buren did not see such an action as necessary or justified.

Van Buren's opposition sent shockwaves through the Democratic Party. Even his old mentor Andrew Jackson could not believe it, initially declaring that the letter must be a forgery. Jackson was so disappointed in his former vice president that he came out of retirement with his own public letter. Arguing that the Texians were "almost unanimous" in their support of annexation and that Mexico had not made a major effort to reoccupy the country, Jackson insisted that Texas must be admitted to the United States. Following the lead of Tyler and Calhoun, Old Hickory warned that if Texas remained independent, it would "inevitably [be] driven into alliances and commercial regulations with the European powers, of a character highly injurious and probably hostile to this country." Jackson went so far as to place Texas at the center of American national security, contending that if Texas did not join the Union, the United States would be unable to resist "foreign interference," as Texas "is the Key to our safety in the south and the West." The former president did make sure to praise his successor's character, and attempted to give Van Buren the benefit of the doubt with a remark that the New Yorker was likely working with old information, but Jackson clearly saw Van Buren's position as a political and strategic mistake.[5] Writing to newspaper editor Francis Blair, Jackson lamented that Van Buren's public opposition made it "impossible" for him to unite the Democratic Party, and he despaired that any other candidate—including Tyler and Calhoun—had the support necessary to achieve victory. In Jackson's mind, the party nomination, and by extension the election, hung on the immediate annexation of Texas, and a "good democrat" had to be selected to get it done.[6]

The split between Jackson and Van Buren foreshadowed the fight that emerged at the Democratic National Convention from May 27-29. Clay had been nominated without opposition at the Whig Convention on May 1, and the Whig platform notably did not mention Texas at all, instead focusing on Clay's priorities: the Whigs' economic agenda and limiting executive power.[7] By contrast Van Buren, although the front-runner, found himself assailed by Southern and expansionist Democrats. Assembling in Baltimore, the Democrats first agreed to reinstate the rule requiring the nominee to be selected by a two-thirds vote of the Convention. This had been the rule in the 1832 and 1835 conventions, but had been dispensed with when Van Buren ran for reelection in 1840.[8] Van Buren's supporters recognized that they had a simple majority and pushed to retain the 1840 rules, yet the "majority was not hard enough." As William Freehling has pointed out, some Northern Democrats realized that should the former president fail to win the nomination, they might secure the nomination for a favorite son from their own states. As a result, while Van Buren's Northern supporters voted for the former president on the first ballot, they split their vote on the rule-change. When combined with the largely Southern anti-Van Buren delegates, it was just enough for the rule change to go through. As summarized by Freehling, "a healthy faction of Northerners plus most Southerners gave the minority section majority control over the nation's majority party."[9]

The two-thirds requirement effectively doomed Van Buren's candidacy. The New Yorker had a healthy 54.9 percent majority on the first ballot with 146 votes, but that was still 31 votes short of the necessary 177. Van Buren would not get such a high total again. Subsequent ballots saw his support steadily dwindle as the Van Burenites sought alternative candidates such as Pennsylvania senator James Buchanan and former Vice President Richard Mentor Johnson. At the same time, no other candidate had enough support to overcome the two-thirds threshold either. Lewis Cass of Michigan, who was a strong advocate of annexation, positioned himself as Van Buren's chief rival, drawing support primarily from Southern delegations and expansionists. Yet even as Cass managed to gain more votes than Van Buren in the later ballots, he never mustered even a simple majority.[10]

With the convention deadlocked, delegates looked for a new candidate who could unite the party's various factions. The ideal choice soon emerged in the form of former Tennessee governor James K. Polk. Another Jackson protégé, he was known as "Young Hickory" in contrast to his mentor and possessed a combination of qualities that few others did: he was a Southern slaveholder known to support both annexation and Van Buren. Indeed, Polk had initially only hoped to be Van Buren's running mate, but his status as a high-profile Southern Democrat who simultaneously backed Van Buren and annexation put him in position to rise to the top of the ticket. On the ninth ballot, Polk won the nomination unanimously.[11]

If Clay's candidacy defined the Whigs as the anti-annexation party, Polk's nomination confirmed the Democrats as the pro-annexation party. Yet for Polk, annexation was only part of a larger commitment to expanding the United States to become a truly continental power. Hence the final resolution of the party's platform not only called for "the reannexation of Texas"—harkening back to the claim that the United States had a prior legal right to Texas—but also "the reoccupation of Oregon."[12] Tying Texas to Oregon, Polk pushed for expansion as a national issue, not a sectional one, and made it the defining feature of his campaign.

The Whigs' initial reaction to Polk was one of confidence and optimism. Clay had been a nationally renowned figure for over three decades. Polk, for all his political accomplishments, was relatively obscure, leading Whigs to adopt the mocking chant of "Who is James K. Polk?"[13] That optimism remained after the failure of the annexation treaty in the Senate appeared to definitively answer the Texas question. Annexation did not, however, go away, remaining a national issue into the summer. As the months dragged on, the confidence Clay and the Whigs had exhibited began to evaporate. Much of the concern for the Whigs came from their lack of support in the South, and Clay clearly felt the pressure as he issued a series of public letters trying to reassure southerners that he was on their side and further explain his opposition to annexation. On July 1, he insisted that he was not supported by abolitionists and asserted that while he personally "could have no objection to the annexation of Texas" he was "unwilling to see the existing Union dissolved or seriously jeoparded for the sake of acquiring Texas."[14] On July 27, he reiterated this position, insisting that "national dishonor, foreign war, and distraction and division at home were too great sacrifices to make for the acquisition of Texas."[15] Unfortunately for Clay, rather than bolstering his support in the South, the letters disheartened Northern supporters while doing little to mollify Southern skeptics. As summarized by Michael Holt, the so-called "Alabama letters" were "among the biggest mistakes of [Clay's] long political career," harming his candidacy and the Whig Party as a whole.[16]

At the same time, the president without a party also was angling to be elected in his own right. Ever since bringing up the possibility of annexation to Webster in October 1841, Tyler had viewed Texas as his ticket to staying in the White House. Using executive patronage, he attempted to build his own third-party coalition of Democrats and disaffected Whigs who might support him. When the Democrats held their convention in Baltimore, Tyler organized his own party convention at the same time in the same city under the name of Jefferson's old Democratic-Republican Party. He also tied his candidacy and the convention itself directly to Texas, adopting the slogan "Tyler and Texas" and making the convention's theme "Reannexation of Texas—Postponement Is Rejection."[17] By holding his convention at the same time as the Democrats, Tyler seemed to be offering himself up to be the compromise candidate should Van Buren's candidacy falter. Tyler later claimed that he had abstained from the Democratic Convention because if he had been a candidate and lost to Van Buren, it would have ended the Texas debate and forced him to support Van Buren's anti-annexation policy, a prospect Tyler found "impossible to do." By staying separate, Tyler insisted, he had effectively pressured the Democrats into supporting an annexationist, contending that they "felt the move. A Texas man or defeat was the choice left,—and they took a Texas man."[18]

Apart from trying to pressure the Democrats into linking themselves with annexation, Tyler used his presidential authority to guarantee it remained a live issue and illustrated that he was ready to pivot from the treaty's defeat. Three days after the Senate rejected the treaty, the president proposed an alternative method to bring Texas into the Union using the Constitution's admissions clause. Under this clause, a simple majority vote of both houses could bring in a new state, a substantially lower bar than the two-thirds Senate majority required for ratifying a treaty.[19] As Congress went out of session a few days later, the resolution proposal lingered and ensured that "the Texas question was far from dead," remaining at the forefront of the American presidential campaign.[20]

Unfortunately for Tyler, it soon became clear that he did not have the support to run for the presidency in his own right. Polk had set himself up as the pro-annexation candidate and could draw on the institutional support of the Democratic Party. To the extent that Tyler had any supporters, staying in the race threatened to marginally split the annexation vote and allow Clay to enter the White House. Interestingly, Jackson counseled Polk not to publicly court Tyler or his supporters, as the number of "Tylers [sic] friends are a mere drop in the buckett [sic]."[21] Yet the Democrats still used backchannels to maneuver Tyler out of the race and consolidate pro-annexation voters behind Polk. In the end, Tyler agreed to drop out so long as he received assurances that his supporters would be brought into the Democratic fold on equal ground, that attacks on him in the Democratic press would stop, and that the party was fully committed to immediate annexation. Once Jackson promised him that these conditions would be met, Tyler agreed to withdraw.[22]

The *Niles National Register* declared Tyler's decision to exit the race as a move "so generally expected, that it surprises no one."[23] Nevertheless, Tyler used his withdrawal to publicly defend his administration, and annexation in particular. He reiterated that it was a policy driven by the national interest, referring to it as "the greatest boon to the country, and the whole country" and "inseparably connected with the interests of every state in the Union, and every interest of the Union." Tyler also went out of his way to highlight that both Van Buren and Clay—the two most prominent opponents of annexation—had sought to annex Texas during their tenures as secretary of state.[24] Once out of the race, Tyler threw his support to Polk, further emphasizing that the presidential election was to be a referendum on annexation.[25] Tyler's commitment to Polk's election becomes especially evident given the fact that despite urging from Calhoun, Tyler declined to call a special session of Congress to debate his annexation resolution on the grounds that it could harm Polk's election.[26] The president thought it better to have the people weigh in on annexation by proxy and then use the energy from that election to push the measure through.

The Americans were not, however, the only ones having an election in 1844. Houston's three-year term was almost up and he was once again barred from running for reelection, leaving the Texian presidency wide open. The potential change in the Texas executive was pointed to by American annexationists as a reason to move faster. As Jackson noted to a correspondent, "Houston and the people of Texas are now united in favour [sic] of annexation. The next President of Texas, may not be so."[27]

The two main candidates for the Texas presidency were Vice President Edward Burleson and Secretary of State Anson Jones. Burleson had broken with Houston and become the focal point for an antiadministration faction supported by former president Lamar. Conversely, Jones represented a continuation of Houston's policies and was supported by the Raven himself.[28] Surprisingly, annexation was not the defining issue between these two candidates, as both adopted a "wait-and-see attitude," indicating support for independence should annexation fail.[29]

Such an attitude is not surprising, as Tyler and the Americans were also waiting for the outcome of the election before delving into the specifics of a new annexation bill, and the diplomatic situation between Texas, Mexico, and the Europeans remained fluid and fast-moving. As Houston had predicted, the annexation treaty's failure put Texas in a precarious position. Santa Anna and the Mexican government were incensed by the attempt to incorporate what they still claimed as Mexican territory into the United States and once again threatened to invade and reconquer the Lone Star Republic. Meanwhile, Britain and France attempted to pressure Mexico into recognizing Texas to remove a major incentive for Texas to join the Union.[30]

As Texas' secretary of state, Jones was at the center of these diplomatic maneuverings and, like Houston, understood the need to steer Texas carefully through the competing ambitions of the stronger powers. Yet annexation was clearly the preferred policy of most Texians, and Jones's apparent aloofness led some to claim that the secretary was secretly opposed to the project. This attack, however, did not stick, and Jones won the Texas presidency with a solid majority on September 2, 1844. Still, he could not aggressively pursue annexation until the Americans finished their own election.[31] The period between the Texian and American elections roughly corresponded with Houston's lame-duck period before Jones assumed office, and as Houston fell ill that fall, the president-elect used those three months between September and December 1844 to assume a greater role in charting Texas' diplomatic future.

The most notable act during this period was Jones's rejection of Britain's "Diplomatic Act." This proposal held that if Mexico continued to refuse to recognize Texas' independence, then Britain and France would break off diplomatic relations with Mexico. Houston ordered Jones to comply with the act and soon after left the capital to recuperate from his illness. Left with an explicit presidential order, Jones took the extraordinary step of simply ignoring it. There were several reasons for this. The first was that despite not yet being inaugurated, Jones believed that the people's trust on how Texas should proceed had already effectively passed from Houston to himself; thus the final decision on such an important matter should rest with him, the incoming president, rather than the outgoing chief executive. Moreover, with Houston out of the capital, Jones saw himself in a "double capacity" as both "acting and elect President." Viewing the act from that position, Jones believed that accepting such a deal would hinder his administration before it even began, restricting his potential policy options.[32] More seriously, Jones feared that accepting recognition from Mexico under these terms would not allow for a truly independent Texas, but rather a Texas under European influence, "directly complicat[ing] our relations & entangl[ing] us with France & England." Yet perhaps the most prominent reason for Jones rejecting the Diplomatic Act was because it might "defeat Annexation altogether, or lead to a War between Europe & America."[33] Independence on unfavorable terms was unacceptable, and until the Americans held their election Jones was unwilling to consent to a deal which might permanently foreclose the possibility of annexation. When Houston returned, he notably did not overrule Jones' action.[34]

With Jones having rejected the Diplomatic Act, the future of annexation rested in the hands of the American electorate. Polk and the Democrats had remained clear and consistent on their support for annexation. Conversely, Clay's Alabama letters had confused his supporters. To annexationists, it was clear that Clay was not with them, but it was no longer clear to anti-annexationists that he was with them either. The difference between the two campaigns certainly influenced the result, which was one of the closest in American history. Carrying fifteen states and winning 170 electoral votes, Polk defeated Clay. Interestingly, unlike the 1840 and 1848 elections, where both the Whig and Democratic candidates were competitive in every region of the country, this time Polk swept the Lower South from South Carolina to Mississippi, the western states of Illinois, Michigan, and Missouri which bordered the American frontier, and the two states directly bordering Texas: Arkansas and Louisiana. In short, Polk won in those states that would be the most interested in westward expansion or the advancement of slavery. Yet despite Polk's stunning Electoral College victory and regional strength in the South and West, the actual popular vote was much closer, with Polk's winning margin being just over 39,000 votes. The Liberty Party candidate James G. Birney, who supported the immediate abolition of slavery and was staunchly opposed to annexation, won 62,000 votes nationwide and likely acted as a spoiler in drawing votes from Clay in New York and Michigan. If only one-third of Birney's 15,000 votes in New York had gone to Clay, the Kentuckian would have won the election.[35] Instead, Polk managed a close victory which Tyler took as "a complete vindication of his own administration," and a sign that the American people endorsed annexation.[36]

Annexation in the Lame Duck

Polk's election energized the annexationists, who, like Tyler, interpreted the Tennessean's victory as an electoral mandate for bringing Texas into the Union immediately. When Congress reassembled in December 1844,

Tyler wasted no time in ensuring that annexation was at the top of the agenda for the lame-duck session. In his final annual message to Congress, Tyler declared that annexation had been "submitted to the ordeal of public sentiment" and that "a controlling majority of the people and a large majority of the States have declared in favor of immediate annexation." In short, Polk's election demonstrated that "it is the will of both the people and the States that Texas shall be annexed to the Union promptly and immediately." To accomplish what Tyler saw as the will of the people, he again recommended Congress annex Texas through a joint resolution of both houses.[37] A week later, South Carolina senator George McDuffie introduced a resolution that largely copied the terms of the treaty that had been rejected six months before, most notably annexing Texas as a territory and assuming its debts.[38]

The use of a congressional resolution to add territory, however, was quite novel. All other territory the United States had acquired in the previous fifty years been added by treaty, following the constitutional process of the president negotiating the treaty followed by ratification by two-thirds of the Senate. Similarly, the admissions clause had only ever been used to add states out of territory already held by the United States. To incorporate territory without a treaty—much less make an entire independent nation part of the Union—had never been attempted before.

Tyler's innovative use of the admissions clause proved to be exceptionally controversial and conflicted with his strict interpretation of the Constitution. That Tyler was deviating from his Jeffersonian principles became particularly apparent when Albert Gallatin, a member of the founding generation who had served as the secretary of the treasury under both Jefferson and Madison, emerged from retirement to denounce the resolution as unconstitutional. In Gallatin's view, an independent nation could only be added to the Union through a treaty or conquest, and the Constitution clearly laid out the provisions for how a treaty could be ratified. Tyler's effort to pass provisions of the treaty under the guise of a congressional resolution was "an undisguised usurpation of power and violation of the Constitution."[39]

Gallatin's constitutional concerns were carried over into the congressional debates, where the opposition was both bipartisan and bisectional. Senator Rufus Choate, an antislavery and anti-annexation Whig from Massachusetts, declared that

> no human being, save one—no man, woman, or child in this Union, or out of this Union, wise or foolish, drunk or sober, was ever heard to breathe one syllable about this power being applicable to the admission of foreign nations, governments, or states. With one exception, till ten months ago, no such doctrine was ever heard of, or even entertained.[40]

Adams similarly declared the resolution an "apoplexy of the Constitution."[41] One Southern Whig, Virginia senator William C. Rives—who had succeeded Tyler in the Senate—argued that to subvert constitutional procedures in this way could have negative ramifications for the South. Specifically, that if the South "were now so blind as to recognize the dispensing power of a mere majority," the precedent would allow "by way of reprisal, a majority in both Houses undertaking to abolish slavery in the District of Columbia . . . an act prohibiting the removal . . . of slaves from State to State," and perhaps even the abolition of slavery by an act of Congress.[42] Antislavery Democrat George Rathbun of New York attacked Tyler and Calhoun personally, accusing the two of hypocrisy for violating their strict constructionist principles and asserting that this proved only the North and Democrats were true defenders of the Constitution.[43]

Despite the opposition from some Northern Democrats, the party had long advocated territorial expansion,[44] and in the case of Texas had committed itself to annexation during the campaign. Having won the election on an annexationist platform, many Democrats now felt bound to carry it out. At the same time, Southern Whigs had not done well in the elections, and many felt pressured to support annexation in order to take care of the issue as quickly as possible and thereby prevent further damage.[45] Representative Alexander Stephens of Georgia went so far as to proclaim that the entire enterprise was little more than "a miserable humbug got up as a ruse to distract the Whig party at the South."[46] While annexation was not designed to target Southern Whiggery, the public pressure on the Southern Whigs proved to be too great for most of them. Georgia representative Robert Toombs expressed the feeling of many Southern Whigs when he wrote to a colleague that while it was unclear if the resolution was constitutional or not, the fact that annexation had popular support convinced him to support it.[47]

Recognizing their difficult position, a small group of Southern Whigs attempted to take ownership of the Texas question and go farther than even Tyler had proposed. Led by Representative Milton Brown of Tennessee, the Southern Whigs proposed that Texas enter the Union not as a territory, but immediately become a state. Their proposal would also allow Texas to create four new states out of its territory, with those south of the 36° 30' parallel—the Missouri Compromise line—to be slave states if they desired.[48] Such a proposal was radical on two counts. First, all other states which had been added to the Union after the original thirteen had started as territories. Indeed, a significant portion of the land acquired in the Louisiana Purchase in 1803 and the Adams-Onís Treaty of 1819 had yet to be integrated into the United States as states. Second, the option to allow Texas to divide itself into as many as five states, most of which would be slave states, would completely destroy the sectional balance in the Senate and give slave states a definitive majority.

Despite the proposal coming from Southern Whigs, it was embraced by the House Democrats, who passed Brown's resolution 120–98 on January 25, 1845. While a few members crossed party lines, the final vote was largely partisan. 112 Democrats and 8 Southern Whigs voted in favor, while 72 Whigs and 26 Democrats were opposed. In other words, "90 percent of the Whigs opposed 81 percent of the Democrats." As summarized by Michael Holt, "the fight over Texas was still predominantly a partisan battle despite its sectional ramifications."[49]

The Senate was similarly bound up in partisanship, but unlike in the House the Whigs still had a narrow majority and used it in having the Whig-controlled Foreign Relations Committee issue a report recommending that the resolution be rejected.[50] To counter Brown's resolution, Missouri senator Thomas Hart Benton introduced a proposal of his own. Benton, who had led the charge against the annexation treaty, was under pressure from both his party and his constituents to shift to the annexationist side, and he sought to ease that pressure without giving in. His proposal—supported by Northern Democrats—

attempted to delay annexation by stipulating that a new Texas treaty be negotiated. Neither Brown's nor Benton's plans, however, had enough support to pass through the closely divided Senate. The gridlock was only broken when Mississippi senator Robert J. Walker leaned into the pending change in administrations and attempted to reconcile the two plans. In Walker's plan, Congress would grant the president the discretion to do one of two things. Either he could offer immediate annexation to Texas—in line with the Brown resolution—or he could reopen treaty negotiations, in line with the Benton proposal. Of course, the president that Walker and his allies expected to exercise this discretion was Polk, not Tyler, an expectation which aided them in convincing senators— particularly recalcitrant Northern Democrats—to support the measure on a partisan basis.[51]

When the final vote came down on February 28, it was Walker's plan that passed, 27–25.[52] Like the House vote, the Senate vote was largely on party lines. Every Senate Democrat—Northern and Southern—voted in favor of the resolution, while nearly every Senate Whig voted against it. The margin of victory came from three Southern Whigs who defected to the pro-annexation side. That the vote broke down along partisan rather than sectional lines—with fifteen Southern Whigs opposing the resolution—suggests that at this point annexation had become a partisan issue rather than a sectional one, with Southern politics only making the important, but marginal, contribution of flipping the three Southern Whigs.[53]

As Tyler was to leave office in a few days, most Democrats who voted for Walker's resolution expected that the president would leave the resolution on the table, allowing for Polk to decide how to proceed when he entered office on March 4. Tyler, however, subverted expectations and asserted his power one more time. Instead of waiting for Polk, Tyler signed the resolution and, on March 3, 1845, his last full day in office and eight years to the day from when Jackson recognized Texas' independence, dispatched Andrew Jackson Donelson—Old Hickory's nephew—to offer Texas immediate annexation.[54] A major reason for this action was Tyler's belief—shared by Calhoun and other members of the cabinet—that further delay could doom the annexation movement. Polk might have been elected on a pro-annexation platform, but the possibility remained that he could reopen negotiations, which would in turn create new complications. Indeed, Calhoun was receiving reports from the American minister to France, William King, that Britain and France remained opposed to annexation and would likely continue their efforts to prevent it.[55] Another round of negotiations would provide the Europeans with the perfect opportunity to interfere and disrupt annexation efforts. But if Tyler acted immediately, such an outcome could be avoided. In possession of congressional approval to annex Texas and the discretion to offer it, the president decided he was not going to waste this opportunity. By acting first, Tyler functionally committed Polk to immediate annexation. When Polk met with his cabinet after the inauguration, he decided not to recall Donelson, but instead affirmed his predecessor's action and followed through on offering immediate annexation.[56]

At the same time that Tyler was pushing the resolution through Congress, Houston was transitioning out of the Texian presidency. In his farewell address, Houston repeated the recommendation he had made in July after the initial treaty failed, arguing that Texas should "maintain her position" and assume that independence would continue into the foreseeable future. Yet even with that pessimistic attitude, Houston also suggested that "if the United States shall open the door" then they should return "to the beloved land from which we have sprung—the land of the broad stripes and bright stars."[57] He repeated this opinion in private to Jackson, telling the old general that

> it is now the duty of the United States to make an advance that cannot be equivocal in its character, and when she opens the door and removes all impediments, it might be well for Texas to accept the invitation. Until that is done, however, I think it becoming on her part to remain as she now is.[58]

After Jones officially became president on December 9, 1844, Houston continued to offer advice, leaving a memorandum laying out the conditions under which annexation should be considered. These included admitting Texas as a territory, assuming Texas' debt or allowing it to retain its public lands, allowing Texas to be divided into more states, and other provisions concerning public liabilities and land claims.[59]

Jones himself maintained the tried-and-true policy of balancing the great powers. While he waited for the American Congress to debate the resolution, he entertained British and French efforts to prevent annexation. In his memoirs, Jones insisted his position was to act "in good faith simply, to all the powers interested, and [I] was not engaged in *exclusive* efforts for annexation. I was certainly laboring for annexation and independence both at the same time."[60] Britain sought to take advantage of this open-mindedness to once again mediate between Texas and Mexico and finally secure Mexican recognition of Texian independence. With the annexation resolution bogged down in debate, Jones accepted the offer and signed an agreement with Britain and France that if Mexico recognized Texas, it would not proceed with annexation. The agreement also gave the Europeans ninety days convince Mexico to agree. Yet soon after agreeing to mediation, Donelson arrived with Tyler's offer of immediate annexation.[61]

Donelson's arrival put Jones in a difficult position. Ashbel Smith, whom Jones had appointed secretary of state, noted that the new president and much of the cabinet were hesitant about annexation, with some cabinet members openly opposing it.[62] Even Houston had concerns about the resolution, telling Donelson that while he was "in favor of annexation" he wanted to ensure that the terms were fair to Texas, and he worried that the resolution's terms *"are dictated* and the *conditions absolute."* He suggested that further negotiations should take place to figure out the details.[63] The people of Texas, however, were very much in favor of accepting the resolution's terms. As word of the offer leaked out, popular demonstrations erupted throughout the republic supporting the proposal and calling for a convention to debate it and draw up a new state constitution. In response, Jones called Congress to convene in June 1845 and soon after called for a convention to meet on July 4.[64] Yet matters were further complicated when, on May 19, Smith and Mexican Foreign Minister Luis Cuervas agreed to a treaty recognizing Texian independence in exchange for not following through on annexation.[65]

With a Mexican treaty and an annexation offer from the United States in hand, Jones was faced with two stark alternatives: independence or annexation. While Jones insisted he was for annexation, comments from Smith suggest that the president at this stage might have preferred independence. Indeed, Jones's action of simply allowing for mediation with Mexico was enough for some annexationists to burn him in effigy.[66] But in the end, Jones "was the representative of the people, not their ruler," and the people overwhelmingly favored annexation.[67] When the Texas Congress assembled on June 28, 1845, Jones sent over both the Mexican treaty and the American resolution. Neither debate took long. The treaty was resoundingly rejected and the resolution unanimously adopted. When the Annexation Convention assembled it also adopted annexation by a 55–1 vote.[68] Thus, if Houston or Jones and his cabinet had concerns about the specific terms of annexation, they had to respect the will of the people as represented in Congress and the Convention. Texas was joining the Union.

The Aftermath of Annexation

Over the next few months, the Texians created a new state constitution, which was ratified by the people and certified by the US Congress. On December 29, 1845, Polk signed legislation officially making Texas the twenty-eighth state in the Union. In February 1846, the transfer of power was completed with the inauguration of James Henderson—Houston's second secretary of state—as governor of Texas. Houston also reentered American national politics after he was overwhelmingly elected as one of Texas' two new senators. Jones, however, did not receive a single vote and bitterly retired from politics.[69] With these positions filled and the state government up and running, the Lone Star Republic had become the Lone Star State.

In the transition to being a state, Texas' national security now became America's national security, and, in line with the promises that Tyler had made to Houston, Polk sent General Zachary Taylor and a detachment of troops to defend Texan territory from Mexican incursions. Although the precise borders between Texas and Mexico remained disputed, Polk pressed for the broadest possible interpretation, insisting that the border was at the Rio Grande. Yet the presence of Taylor and American troops in disputed territory, along with what turned out to be Mexico's completely justified fear that annexation was a prelude to further American expansion, eventually resulted in a skirmish where

American troops were killed and captured.[70] Polk claimed that "Mexico has passed the boundary of the United States, has invaded our territory and shed American blood upon the American soil" and pushed for Congress to declare war.[71] Two days later, Congress did just that, with now-Senator Houston voting in favor.

In his speech supporting Polk, Houston confirmed what opponents of annexation had warned about—that by annexing Texas the United States was "placed precisely in the situation in which Texas had been for the last ten years": a de facto state of war with Mexico.[72] For Houston, hostilities between Mexican and American forces had not started in 1846 but had simply been carried over from the lingering fighting that had begun with the Texas Revolution in 1835.

The end result of the Mexican War was that the United States expanded to the Pacific Ocean, gaining territory that became California, Nevada, Utah, and parts of Arizona, New Mexico, Colorado, and Wyoming. Combined with the organization of the Oregon Territory under Polk, the United States now spanned the North American continent. The addition of Texas had energized America's movement west to become a truly continental power. Yet this expansion of territory also exacerbated the sectional crisis over slavery, laying the groundwork for the coming Civil War.

Houston and Tyler after Annexation

Serving in the Senate until 1859, Houston became a prominent Unionist who sought to balance sectional tensions. He voted for the Compromise of 1850, which attempted to address the organization of the new western territories acquired in the Mexican War in a way that satisfied both the North and the South. Four years later, he voted against the Kansas-Nebraska Act that allowed the western territories to decide for themselves whether or not they would have slavery. Having once been considered Jackson's heir apparent, the former Texian president also sought the American presidency several times, pursuing the Democratic Party nomination in 1852, and then—after leaving the party in response to the Kansa-Nebraska Act in 1854—running for the nominations of the American Party—more famously known as the "Know Nothings"—in

1856 and the Constitutional Union Party in 1860. Despite his previous presidential experience, he failed to win any party's nomination. He did, however, become governor of Texas in 1859, becoming the only man to serve as governor of two different states.[73]

Unlike Houston, Tyler did not have much of a political career after leaving the presidency. Scorned by both parties, he had no firm political base, and while he sometimes considered running again for the presidency, such plans never got off the ground.[74] Instead, Tyler spent much of his retirement in the 1840s and 1850s defending his administration, and, more specifically, taking credit for annexing Texas. Interestingly, it was in the fight for credit that Tyler and Houston had their most public correspondence.[75] In 1847, Tyler published a public letter asserting his primary role in adding Texas to the Union—countering contrary claims made by Calhoun—and insisting that he pursued annexation partially in response to "*authentic* information that other nations were exerting all their efforts to induce a course of action on the part of Texas, at war ... with the permanent interests of the United States."[76]

Houston objected to this characterization and in his own public letter accused the United States of treating Texas "with coldness, reserve or palpable discouragement." The former Texian president further argued that the Americans' initial hostility to annexation forced him to find other methods by which to secure independence, including "a treaty with some power, defensive against Mexico." Even with this admission, Houston maintained that Tyler's suggestion that Texas was being manipulated by other nations to damage the United States was nothing more than warped "phantasies and conjured up notions of intrigues, which had existence only in imagination." Houston also expressed a kind of familial devotion in insisting that rather than Tyler, Calhoun, or even himself, it was Jackson who should be credited with leading the way on annexation.[77]

Incensed by Houston's retort, Tyler responded with another public letter where he commented that his Texian counterpart had "*coquetted with England.*" While he was willing to believe that Houston had "merely indulged in the course of innocent flirtation, in order to awaken the jealousies of the people of the United States," it appeared to be more than that given that Texas had used British mediation to attempt to gain recognition from Mexico. Tyler also pushed back on Houston's insistence that Jackson was the driving force, writing that he "took the initiative without any previous consultation with that distinguished man."[78]

With each man's pride now involved, Houston proclaimed that his responsibility had been to act "on behalf of Texas," and since "she met no encouragement from her most natural friend, the United States, she would have to look for aid and succor to some other quarter," including Europe. Going further, Houston noted that while Tyler eventually took some initiative in pursuing annexation, it did not happen until 1843. In Houston's view, such a delay made Tyler the real coquette, holding out to Texas the possibility of annexation without taking firm steps towards it until two years into his presidency. More seriously, Houston contended that the promises Tyler's administration had made concerning military aid and protection for Texas during the annexation debate raised serious questions about Tyler being a "wilful [sic] and flagrant violator of the constitution." Specifically, Houston highlighted that Tyler had committed military forces to aid Texas without the approval of Congress. Such criticisms were not new, but it is interesting to see Houston, who had asked for those reassurances, raise these constitutional points. For his part, Houston argued that his position required him to look out for the best interests of Texas and "to obtain for her all the advantages of security and protection." Whether those advantages were in line with the American constitution was not, at that point, his responsibility.[79]

Other individuals jumped into the fray after this back-and-forth in the press, but both presidents stopped after their second letter and reconciled several years later.[80] In 1860, however, they found themselves on opposite sides of the greatest crisis in American history: the Civil War.

Houston was governor of Texas when Southern states began seceding in response to Abraham Lincoln's election to the presidency. As such, he was positioned to be directly involved in determining how Texas would respond. Although he was no fan of Lincoln, Houston opposed the secessionists and pushed for Texas to remain true to the Union, telling a mass meeting that "The Union is worth more than Mr. Lincoln, and if the battle is to be fought for the Constitution, let us fight it in the Union and for the sake of Union."[81] He had been willing to fight for independence from Mexico when he believed his constitutional rights had been violated, but he did not believe that had happened in the United States and could not justify separation. When a convention called by the Texas legislature voted to secede on February 1, 1861, Houston dutifully recognized Texas as independent of the United States, but insisted that Texas had simply "assume[d] the nationality with which she parted on entering the Union."[82] The man who had fought for Texas' annexation now presided over its secession. Yet even while Houston was willing to go along with declaring Texas an independent republic again, he did not consent to Texas joining the Confederacy. In his view, the convention which had voted on secession only had the authority to withdraw from the Union, not to join a new one. When Houston refused to take an oath of allegiance to the Confederacy, the governorship was declared vacant, and Houston's political career was over. He died two years later on July 26, 1863.[83]

In Tyler's case, the secession crisis breathed new life into his political career as he reentered politics as the only living former president from the South. Like Houston, Tyler had opposed Lincoln during the election, telling his son that "the defeat of Lincoln was the great matter at issue, and that all others were subordinate."[84] After Lincoln won and the Southern states started seceding, Tyler proposed a convention of delegates from the border states—six free and six slave—to find a compromise that might end the crisis. The former president believed that only the border states would be moderate enough to find a reasonable solution apart from what he viewed as the extremists in the North and South. The Virginia legislature, however, altered the proposal to be a convention of all the states—much to Tyler's annoyance—and appointed Tyler to represent the Old Dominion.[85]

When the Washington Peace Conference met on February 4, 1861— three days after Texas had voted to secede—Tyler was elected its presiding officer and set to work trying to find a compromise. After three weeks of often unproductive and raucous debate, the conference's proposal was a constitutional amendment that was quite similar to other compromise amendments which had previously failed in Congress. The amendment would have extended the Missouri Compromise line to the Pacific, banned any future amendments abolishing slavery, reinforced the Constitution's existing fugitive slave clause, banned the international slave trade—which had already been banned by legislation in 1808—in perpetuity, and enshrined the Constitution's three-fifths clause so it could not be amended without the unanimous consent of the states.[86] Tyler opposed the compromise as not doing enough to protect Southern interests, supporting an alternative amendment that would have given the South a veto on appointments south of the Missouri Compromise line. Nonetheless, he dutifully forwarded the proposal to Congress, where it was ignored.[87]

During the conference, Tyler and other delegates also met with President-elect Lincoln, and it was this meeting that seems to have solidified Tyler's decision to become a secessionist. In the meeting, Lincoln reiterated his campaign promise not to expand slavery into the territories and implied that war might be necessary if the South did not return to the Union. The former president took the future president at his word. When he was appointed as a delegate to the Virginia State Convention which would decide whether Virginia would secede, the elder statesman spoke out in favor of secession.[88] Initially, the Convention disagreed with Tyler, voting down secession 90–45 on April 4. But after shots were fired at Fort Sumter and Lincoln called for raising 75,000 Union troops, the delegates met again and voted to secede 88–55, with Tyler in the majority.[89]

After voting to secede from the United States, the seventy-one-year-old Tyler was selected to lead the commission that negotiated Virginia's entry into the Confederacy and helped secure Richmond, Virginia as the capital of the Confederate States. He was also selected to represent Virginia in the Provisional Confederate Congress and soon after was elected to a term in the Confederate House of Representatives. The president-turned-secessionist died on January 18, 1862, while waiting for the first session to begin.[90]

It is ironic that the two men who worked most strenuously to add Texas to the Union died in states attempting to leave it. Of course, the manner by which they left the United States was quite different. Houston, the hero of San Jacinto who had bestridden Texas politics like a colossus since the Revolution, saw his public life unceremoniously ended against his will due to his personal devotion to the Union. By contrast, Tyler, the president without a party, saw his political fortunes rejuvenated as the Union collapsed. When he died, the Confederacy celebrated him as a hero with a state funeral and procession attended by Confederate President Jefferson Davis and other luminaries of the Confederate government. But in the Union Tyler had presided over, he was castigated as a traitor.[91] Despite the different circumstances of their deaths, Tyler and Houston irrevocably changed the United States through their work to annex Texas, and in doing so illustrated some of the nuances of executive power in an American-style constitutional system.

CONCLUSION

The Primacy of Presidential Policymaking

From the beginning, the annexation of Texas was driven by presidents. Going back to Jefferson's claim that Texas was included in the Louisiana Purchase, all the way to Polk overseeing Texas' transition into a state, American policy towards Texas was directed at the presidential level. Similarly, while annexation was popular among the Texians, it was the Texian presidents deciding whether or not to pursue it. The initial proposal and its withdrawal were both commanded by Houston. Mirabeau Lamar's decision to reorient Texian policy towards a vision of a permanently independent Texas was his alone, as was Houston's decision to give annexation another try in his second term.

How Tyler and Houston addressed the many complicating factors which affected annexation, and the ways in which those factors influenced their decision-making, can be clearly seen when we examine the two presidents side by side and assess their differing structural, constitutional, and political positions.

Structural Differences

In 1836, Houston found himself in a situation more analogous to George Washington in 1789 than to Jackson or Tyler: governing a weak young republic surrounded by stronger powers. His agency in pursuing annexation, therefore, was largely dependent on what those larger powers would accept. The United States unilaterally dismissed Texas' requests for annexation repeatedly, even forcing Houston to withdraw its annexation request to preserve Texas' international reputation as an independent republic. Moreover, Houston had to balance his efforts with how Mexico, Britain, and France would react, even declining Tyler's first attempt to open negotiations because it might create animosity with those other powers. In essence, Texas' general weakness severely limited Houston's options. Yet it is within those constraints that Houston revealed himself to be a surprisingly astute grand strategist. In spite of the United States' delay in responding to his annexation requests, Houston engaged with Britain and France in a manner that simultaneously bolstered Texian independence against additional hostile actions by Mexico and stoked American fears of European interference in North America, eventually inducing the Tyler administration to finally act.

Texas' vulnerable position may have also allowed Houston more expansive opportunities to exercise executive power. For its entire lifespan, the Republic of Texas was under existential threat from Mexico, enduring several incursions from Mexican forces. This danger was even acknowledged by the Texas Congress, as it was willing to grant Houston near dictatorial powers to respond to the emergency. While Houston declined those powers, such an action clearly illustrates that Congress trusted him with broad discretion and was not adversarial enough to impose strict limits, rather granting him a large amount of leeway. Much of this may be due to Houston's personal popularity and political support, yet it also reflects a long-standing dictum of Anglo-American political thought: that a single energetic executive is best positioned to respond to what Alexander Hamilton called "the most critical emergencies of the state."[1] The English philosopher John Locke went so far as to say that executives may even need to employ what he called prerogative power and "act according to discretion, for the public good, without the prescription of the law, and sometimes even against it."[2] Whether American presidents have such prerogative power and how that power operates in a constitutional system remains a major issue of scholarly debate,[3] but Houston's rejection of that authority on constitutional grounds indicates that he did not think such emergency authority was inherent in the Texas constitution. Nevertheless, the Texian president's example reinforces the observation that even in the absence of clear prerogative actions, existential threats and the necessities of national security contribute to the expansion of executive power as legislatures give executives a wide berth to act to ensure the survival of the political community.

Relatedly, Houston's veto of the Texas Congress' declaration of war against Mexico is a reminder that even as Congress is the branch designated to declare war—in both the American and Texian constitutions—the president's role in the legislative process and position as commander in chief ensures that he will be consulted before war is declared. As there is no instance in American history of a president vetoing a declaration of war, Houston provides an instructive example that might be applied to American practice whereby Congress declares a war that the president opposes and what outcome we might expect to see in such an inter-branch dispute. In this case, the president's legislative and military roles allowed him to single-handedly block a formal declaration of war, indicating that the president's constitutional power in declaring war may be more significant than previously thought.

The internal strength of the different governments serves as another point of departure. Reflecting on his first term, Houston wrote to Jackson that while the latter "had an organized Government, and men who were accustomed to civil rule," he "had to command a Government from chaos, with men who had never been accustomed as a community, to any rule, but their passions, or to any government, but their will."[4] Compared to the enlightened statesmen of the American Founding—or even luminaries like Jackson, Clay, Webster, and Calhoun who shaped antebellum America—Texas' Founding Fathers were rough and rustic. The few who had political and military experience quickly assumed leadership positions—as is clear from Houston's meteoric rise—yet the rest of the Texas government was filled out by political neophytes, most of whom had moved to Texas simply to make a new start. Anson Jones, for example, had been a failed doctor and businessman before "drift[ing] into Texas, penniless, intent only upon making a new start, ambitious only to pay off his debts, resolved only to avoid involvements of every kind."[5]

For a man like Houston, the lack of experienced political leadership had both benefits and drawbacks. On the positive side, it allowed Houston to be the proverbial "big fish in a small pond." A political veteran of Congress and a former governor, Houston dominated Texas politics in a way that he would not have been able to in Washington or even in his home state of Tennessee. Indeed, once he was thrust back into American politics, he was not even able to win a party's presidential nomination, much less the presidency itself. On the negative side, Texas' relatively small size and the inexperience of the Lone Star Republic's politicians highlights one of the detriments of the small republic discussed by James Madison in *Federalist 10*, in that "unworthy candidates" might achieve political prominence.[6] The disastrous presidency of Mirabeau Lamar seems to have borne out that observation.

Conversely, Tyler's agency was not hindered by the structural position of the United States. Despite his own difficult political situation, Tyler could afford to wait to move on annexation until the political conditions were right and he was not dependent on the actions of Texas, Britain, Mexico, or any other power. While Tyler did have to wait a few months before Texas consented to negotiations in the spring of 1844, it was not the eight years Houston had endured. Similarly, although Houston's diplomacy with the Europeans was a major factor in compelling Tyler to act, the underlying reason for his feeling of compulsion was markedly different from that felt by Houston. For Tyler, annexing Texas was in the national interest, but failure to do so did not pose an existential threat to the survival of the Union. Rather, his concern about British interference with Texas was about great power politics. Adhering to the principles of the Monroe Doctrine, Tyler and his administration did not want Britain or any other European power to gain a greater foothold in North America, particularly in the Southwest, which might block further expansion. It was a manifestation of the United States' position as an emerging world power seeking to protect its sphere of influence from outside intervention.

Ironically, even as the United States' superior position as a rising power allowed Tyler to pursue annexation according to his own discretion, the lack of an existential threat constrained his exercise of executive power. For the Texians, annexation was central to whether Texas would survive as a political entity, a fact which allowed Houston relatively free reign in annexation policy. For the United States, however, annexation was a debatable policy issue. As the stakes were comparatively lower, Congress had more agency in pushing back and limiting Tyler's activities, and the president was unable to make any claims to emergency powers which might have enabled him to circumvent those limitations.

Constitutional Variance

Fortunately for Tyler, the American presidency's constitutional authority was still quite robust, and it was the Texian presidency which was generally more restricted in its constitutional powers. The drawbacks of the Texas constitution's limited executive are particularly evident in the frequent presidential turnover and lack of administrative stability fostered by the shorter three-year terms and the bar on presidents running for consecutive terms. By having a presidential term limit—and limiting Houston's first term to only two years—Texas was unable to develop a consistent approach to annexation. Instead, annexation policy whipped from the pro-annexation Houston to the anti-annexation Lamar and back again. Nor did it have the intended effect of preventing one man from accumulating substantial political power. Houston was elected to the Texas House of Representatives in between his presidential terms, shifting his personal faction from the executive to the legislative branch and enabling him to continue having a major voice in policy matters. Had Houston served consecutive terms, it is possible that he could have kept up steady pressure on the United States or instituted his surreptitious alliance with the Europeans earlier in a way that might have elicited a positive reaction from the United States. Avoiding the debacles of the Lamar administration would have also placed Texas in a better military and economic position and given Houston a stronger hand when attempting to deter Mexico and negotiate with the United States.

While the American presidency also saw turnover in the executive office during this period, it was not driven by constitutional factors. Jackson voluntarily chose to retire after two terms, while Van Buren lost the election of 1840 and Harrison died in office. Notably, Tyler's nearly four-year term proved to be just long enough to both reorient American foreign policy towards Texas and conclude annexation. Despite substantial turnover at the cabinet level—particularly with three secretaries of state[7]—Tyler remained on top of the administration and maintained his support for annexation, waiting until the opportune political moment and the right personnel to shift course. Indeed, Tyler's actions are an almost perfect illustration of how Hamilton anticipated the office's four-year term and potential for reelection would incentivize presidents to act. In regard to the former, Tyler's longer term enabled him to push for annexation even when it was politically unpalatable, giving the people "time and opportunity for more cool and sedate reflection."[8] Once the people had a chance to express their support in the election of 1844, Tyler utilized that popular energy to push the measure through. With the latter, Tyler saw Texas as his ticket to being elected in his own right, and his own "love of fame" prompted him "to plan and undertake extensive and arduous enterprises" for what he saw as beneficial for the public. Despite Tyler ultimately failing as a presidential candidate, the motivation provided by the possibility of being elected to his own term encouraged him to pursue annexation as a signature policy victory and see it through in his final days in office to avoid "commit[ing the work] to hands which might be unequal or unfriendly to the task."[9]

Apart from the effects that emerged out of each presidency's differing constitutional structures, the powers utilized by the presidents were largely the same. With their treaty powers, Tyler and Houston were positioned to be the primary actors in their nations' foreign policies, and each directed their country's diplomacy to emphasize annexation. At various times both attempted to employ their presidency's "first-mover advantage," unilaterally initiating annexation negotiations with the other and "establish[ing] an antecedent state of things" before the other branches, or even other governments, could react.[10] Their ability to use their authority effectively, however, was limited by their circumstances. Houston's repeated attempts to begin negotiations were stonewalled by the United States until Tyler finally felt he could act, at which point he became the first mover by reaching out to Texas. Yet even when Houston was blocked by political considerations in the United States, he was still able to engage with the Europeans to entice the Americans into action, activities that Tyler was well aware of and responsive to because of his constitutional position as head of the American diplomatic corps. Conversely, Houston was able to get the treaty ratified by the Texas Senate, whereas Tyler failed to get it ratified by the American Senate, illustrating the limits of the treaty power and the role politics plays in enforcing constitutional restrictions.

When it came to personnel, Tyler was initially hamstrung because he inherited his cabinet from Harrison rather than constructing his own. Even after the mass cabinet resignation that initiated his expulsion from the Whig Party, Tyler knew that he needed to retain Daniel Webster as secretary of state to preserve his political standing. Yet Webster's staunch opposition to annexation severely inhibited the president's pursuit of it, resulting in Tyler having to convince Webster to resign in order to proceed. Although he had the constitutional power to simply remove Webster, such an action likely would have caused substantial political blowback, as Whig Party doctrine opposed presidents unilaterally removing cabinet members.[11] While Tyler was not afraid to utilize the removal power throughout his presidency, including for other cabinet members, his expulsion from the Whig Party, the conflicting interpretations of the removal power, and the potential fallout from firing a high-profile figure like Webster made matters significantly more complicated.

For the Texians, no such doubt existed. The Texas constitution was clear that the Senate had to consent to presidential removals, although given Houston's personal popularity and political clout such consent likely would not have been hard to get. Moreover, Houston did not utilize the removal power for major diplomatic subordinates like Jones and Smith, as they largely agreed with him on his policy measures. The only time where the senatorial consent requirement might have been a major restraint on Houston was when Jones ignored the president's command to carry out Britain's "Diplomatic Act" and Houston declined to remove him. While Houston did not comment on why he allowed Jones' decision to stand, it may have been because it would have been difficult to get senatorial consent to remove Jones. Alternatively, Houston may have been convinced Jones was right or moved past it because Jones was already the president-elect. In either case, that this is the main instance where Houston may have been constrained by the Texas constitution's removal power provision illustrates how his popularity enabled him to overcome that technical restraint. Had the positions been reversed, and the American constitution clearly required senatorial consent for removals, Tyler's control over his administration would have been significantly diminished. It was only once Tyler had subordinates who agreed with his pro-annexation policy that he was able to engage with Houston and work towards a common goal.

Constitutional Innovations and Precedents

Along with recognizing the constitutional powers utilized, we must also see how these presidents, specifically Tyler, engaged in constitutional interpretation and set precedents which would be adopted by later presidents seeking to annex territory. We see this on two levels.

First, in response to Houston's insistence on a promise of military assistance, Tyler determined that he had the authority as commander in chief to command American forces to be ready to assist the Texians in the event of Mexican retaliation and use statutorily provided secret service funds to finance those operations. Such an action fell into the gray area between the president's military powers and Congress's power of the purse. The secret service funds had been appropriated by Congress, but Tyler's use of them for actions that could have sparked a war with Mexico was constitutionally questionable.[12] Houston himself questioned the constitutional legitimacy of these actions after annexation was accomplished, publicly accusing Tyler of being a "wilful [sic] and flagrant violator of the constitution."[13] It is notable, however, that Houston was not overly concerned about constitutional propriety at the time. His concern was for the Texas constitution, not its antecedent, and his institutional position as president of Texas oriented him to seek his policy goals regardless of their constitutionality under the American constitution. Nevertheless, Tyler was not deterred by such constitutional concerns, either at the time or afterward. He determined that he had the statutory authorization to use those funds for purposes that fell under his military and diplomatic authority, a determination that proved critical to securing Texas' consent.

This expansive interpretation of the president's military authority was adopted roughly twenty-five years later by President Ulysses S. Grant. In 1869, Grant hoped to annex the Dominican Republic—then known as Santo Domingo—to give the United States a naval foothold in the Caribbean, grant Americans access to its natural resources, and create a new "black American frontier" for newly freed African Americans to escape racial persecution.[14] During the treaty negotiations, Grant adopted Tyler's tactic of employing the military to protect Santo Domingo from invasion and provide assurances to the Dominican government. While the Senate ultimately voted down the treaty, it upheld Grant's military actions—and by extension Tyler's interpretation of the president's commander in chief powers—as legitimate.[15]

Second, Tyler's interpretation of the admissions clause as applying to foreign states and as a method to annex Texas after the treaty failed was innovative in employing a frequently used clause in a novel way. While it generated significant questions regarding its constitutionality, the fact that a hostile Congress accepted that interpretation and annexed Texas suggests that despite those worries, it was ultimately determined to be a legitimate constitutional process for incorporating a foreign nation into the United States. It also set a precedent which was utilized by President William McKinley when he attempted to annex the Republic of Hawaii.

The United States' diplomatic relationship with Hawaii began during the Tyler administration when the president unilaterally recognized the independent Kingdom of Hawaii and expanded the Monroe Doctrine into the Pacific, a change which came to be known as the Tyler Doctrine.[16] Over fifty years later, President Benjamin Harrison—the grandson of Tyler's predecessor—made the first effort to annex Hawaii after its monarch, Queen Liliʻuokalani, was overthrown in a coup d'état led by American-descended Hawaiians. Harrison negotiated an annexation treaty with the new provisional government, but the Senate did not act on it before Harrison left office in March 1893. His successor, Grover Cleveland, opposed annexation and withdrew the treaty, settling into regular diplomatic relations with what soon became the Republic of Hawaii.[17]

When Cleveland left office in 1897, annexation became a live possibility again, as the new President William McKinley was, like Tyler and Polk before him, an expansionist. McKinley even used the same language that had been employed regarding Texas, telling an aide that annexing Hawaii "is manifest destiny."[18] Yet also like Tyler and Texas, the Senate rejected McKinley's annexation treaty. Taking a page out of Tyler's book, McKinley and his allies turned to a joint resolution to bring

Hawaii in as a territory, and congressional committees in both houses cited Tyler's Texas resolution as a precedent. In July 1898, Congress passed the joint resolution and annexed Hawaii.[19] Tyler's constitutional innovation in using congressional resolutions to add territory was no longer a one-time quirk borne out of political necessity but a legitimate method for constitutionally expanding the territory of the United States.

In short, Tyler and Houston not only demonstrated the limits and possibilities that emerge from their distinct constitutional positions, but also the ways presidents may contribute to constitutional interpretation and construction, even developing new constitutional methods for pursuing their policy goals.

Political Contexts

With regard to their political contexts, Tyler and Houston could not have been more different. As the first vice president to become president upon the death of his predecessor, Tyler faced legitimacy questions from the beginning of his tenure, with opponents claiming that he was merely an "Acting" President and derisively referring to him as "His Accidency." As a result, Tyler could not leverage his personal popularity to pursue his goals, as he did not really have any personal popularity. By contrast, Houston was a popular war hero who had been overwhelmingly elected to the Texas presidency twice. Moreover, unlike his American contemporaries who were indirectly elected through the Electoral College, Houston had been elected directly by the people, granting him a stronger claim to be their direct representative.

At a broader institutional level, the party systems of the United States and Texas were also quite different. The Whig and Democratic Parties which dominated American politics in the 1830s and 1840s "provided a substantial amount of procedural and administrative order during the antebellum period."[20] Thus, for Tyler to be expelled from the Whigs and rebuked by the Democrats meant that in addition to lacking any partisan support, he was stripped of many of the administrative supports antebellum presidents normally relied on. As a president without a party during an exceptionally partisan era, Tyler was left isolated and forced to rely solely on his constitutional powers to achieve his goals.

The lack of party support also had major implications for Tyler's relationship with Congress. Without a friendly coalition, Tyler usually failed to gain Congress' cooperation, as shown by the initial failure of the annexation treaty. This forced him to prioritize policy goals which were more politically palatable over annexation, at least until the political situation appeared more amenable. That Tyler was eventually able to move on the issue and get the joint resolution through Congress speaks to his timing and tenacity in continuing to press for annexation. Yet his efforts were also aided by Polk's election highlighting popular support for the measure. Moreover, the election had made annexation into a partisan issue. With those changes in circumstances, Tyler was able to leverage that electoral energy and partisan support to get annexation passed by a very hostile Congress.

Conversely, Houston did not face the institutionalized opposition of two major political parties because Texas did not have organized political parties. In the personalized politics of Texas, Houston became the sun Texas politics revolved around. As one member of the Texas Congress later reflected, "Texas had nothing to do with parties in the United States. We were Sam Houston or anti–Sam Houston,"[21] and the pro-Houston side had a notable edge. In such an environment, Houston had fewer political constraints impeding him from his policy goals.

The differing norms surrounding each presidency also affected the ways in which Tyler and Houston pursued annexation. As Jeffrey Tulis has pointed out, the norm for nineteenth-century presidents was that they not make public speeches on policy issues. Instead, presidential rhetoric was meant to be institutional and directed to Congress in the form of annual addresses or veto messages. While some presidents might use those events to communicate with the people and turn public opinion to their side, they were still constrained by the institutional nature of that rhetoric, as they were not addressing the people directly.[22] Tyler remained within the bounds of this norm, and so his public statements on annexation were not directly to the people, but were contained within his annual messages or put out through the administration's partisan newspaper, the *Madisonian*.[23] This norm, however, did not apply to former or prospective presidents, as Jackson, Van Buren, and Clay all made public statements on annexation, primarily through public letters published in newspapers. It also does not seem to have applied to the Texian presidency, as Houston routinely made public speeches on policy issues, including annexation. That Houston was able to make such appeals without censure points to the Texian presidency not being held to the same expectations regarding popular rhetoric, as well as to its plebiscitary nature and the closer connection between the president and the Texian people. By virtue of their popular election and smaller electorate, Texian presidents were positioned to make direct popular appeals to their constituents. While such direct appeals were rare and frowned upon in the nineteenth century, they became and remain routine for American presidents in the twentieth and twenty-first centuries. Thus, we can view Houston's decision to "go public"[24] while president as anticipating this development in American presidential rhetoric.

How annexation fit into the general politics of Texas and the United States was also significantly different. Nearly from the moment they gained independence, the Texians supported annexation, voting overwhelmingly in favor of it in the 1836 referendum and giving Houston a policy mandate for his first administration. The drift by some Texians away from annexation, and even Houston's efforts seeking support from the British and the French to sustain an independent Texas, emerged primarily because of American resistance, not out of a deep-seated desire for an independent Texian republic. Particularly after Lamar's disastrous anti-annexation administration, few supported Texas remaining independent except as a second choice if the Americans persisted in saying no.

The popular support for annexation, as well as Houston's personal reputation, resulted in little domestic opposition to the measure within Texas. Whatever hesitation there was seemed to be concentrated among some of the Texian elite, such as Jones's last cabinet. Yet popular support for annexation was too strong even for those holdouts. As summarized by Stanley Siegel, "the annexation of Texas was therefore effected by the people of the Republic and not their elected officials."[25] Just as Polk's election helped sway wavering members of Congress to ultimately vote for annexation, popular opinion in Texas effectively forced reluctant leaders to carry out annexation even under terms they viewed as less than ideal.

In the United States, however, annexation was only a part of the changing political and sectional dynamics of antebellum America. Prior to the Texas Revolution, the acquisition of Texas was not a partisan or exceptionally divisive issue and had support from presidents across the political spectrum. The archrivals Adams and Jackson—as well as their attendant Secretaries of State Clay and Van Buren, respectively—had all sought to purchase Texas from Mexico during their time in office. Yet after Texas won its independence, the politics of annexation became embroiled in the United States' growing sectional conflict. The development of the abolitionist movement and Southern slaveholders' pivot to making positive arguments for slavery in the 1830s created a political environment that made the incorporation of a slave republic—particularly one as large as Texas—untenable for national politicians seeking to balance sectional interests. Thus, Jackson could not risk pursuing annexation, or even recognition, of Texas during the 1836 election for fear it would divide the Democratic Party and doom Van Buren's election to the presidency. Only after Van Buren was safely elected did Jackson take the tentative step of recognizing Texian independence. While in office, Van Buren was similarly restrained due to his concern with maintaining party unity and not fanning the incipient sparks of sectional strife into a larger conflagration. By contrast, after his presidency Adams turned completely against annexation and became one of its staunchest opponents in Congress. When the treaty was signed in 1844, Van Buren and Clay joined the chorus of opposition decrying Tyler's efforts. The turn by these men against annexation is indicative of the major changes in American politics that made Texas' admission to the Union a far more controversial question with major implications for the United States' growing sectional divide.

Even Tyler's internal administration was initially hindered by these sectional politics insofar as Webster and Everett opposed annexation. Only when the southerners Upshur and Calhoun came to lead the State Department could the president finally approach the issue, yet those same southerners exacerbated the sectional problem. For despite Tyler's repeated insistence on the national benefits of annexing Texas, his subordinates, particularly Calhoun, based their arguments around the explicitly Southern argument of defending and advancing slavery, aggravating sectional tensions rather than diffusing them.

Assessing Tyler and Houston

Comparing the presidents in these different contexts, we can see how the diverse situations surrounding them affected their approach, decision-making, and actions regarding Texas' annexation. For Houston, the primary challenge came not from internal opposition or lack of popular support, but from external threats. As a small and weak new nation, Houston was subject to the whims of greater powers and was forced to be far more strategic in employing his diplomatic authority to navigate through competing American, European, and Mexican interests. That he was able to do so speaks to his personal talent as an administrator and diplomat, as well as to the powers of the Texian presidency, which in foreign policy were practically identical to those held by the American executive.

Conversely, Tyler's problems were domestic. An unelected president without a party coalition facing a hostile Congress and sectional tension, Tyler had to rely almost solely on executive actions to pursue annexation. Considering his intensely constrained circumstances it is remarkable that Tyler was able to make any progress at all, and his success is a testament to the American presidency's robust constitutional powers. This is particularly true in foreign policy as Tyler unilaterally pivoted towards Texas and continued advocating for annexation even after the initial treaty failed. His ability to find a new avenue for achieving annexation and leverage Polk's victory also illuminates the ways in which even unelected lame-duck presidents can exercise the office's considerable energy and agency.

With their unique challenges, both cases illustrate how constitutional presidential power, particularly in foreign policy, can be utilized effectively despite external obstacles and internal obstruction in radically different environments. While they had to use their powers differently to meet their varied circumstances, each president still possessed the authority they needed to be successful. Moreover, each president was the prime mover in initiating and driving annexation policy, making it a priority and unilaterally orienting their nation's foreign policy to achieve it.

You could not have two presidents in more dissimilar political situations than John Tyler and Sam Houston. But in studying them together and examining the Texian presidency as a variant of the American original, they show the range of the presidency's constitutional powers and demonstrate that regardless of a president's internal or external circumstances, the office possesses the agency and capacity to achieve significant policy goals.

NOTES

ABBREVIATIONS

CAJ   *Correspondence of Andrew Jackson*, ed. John Spencer Bassett Washington, D.C.: Carnegie Institution of Washington, 1929.

DCRT   *Diplomatic Correspondence of the Republic of Texas*. Washington: Government Printing Office, 1908.

DCUS   *Diplomatic Correspondence of the United States: Inter-American Affairs, 1831–1860*, ed. William R. Manning. Washington: Carnegie Endowment for International Peace, 1936.

DTH   *Documents of Texas History*, ed. Ernest Wallace, David M. Vigness, and George B. Ward. Austin, TX: State House Press, 1994.

PJCC   *The Papers of John C. Calhoun*, ed. Clyde N. Wilson and Shirley Bright Cook. Columbia, SC: University of South Carolina Press, 1987.

TLT   *The Laws of Texas, 1822–1897*, comp. H.P.H. Gammel. Austin, TX: Gammel Book Company, 1898.

WSH   *The Writings of Sam Houston, 1813–1863*, ed. Amelia W. Williams and Eugene C. Barker. Austin, TX: The University of Texas Press, 1939.

INTRODUCTION: NOT ONE, BUT TWO PRESIDENTS

1. Julius W. Pratt, "The Origin of 'Manifest Destiny,'" *American Historical Review* 32, no. 4 (July 1927): 795–798. For the original use of this phrase in context see John O'Sullivan, "Annexation," *United States Magazine and Democratic Review* 17, no. 1 (July–August 1845): 5–10.

2. William W. Freehling, *The Road to Disunion: Secessionists at Bay, 1776–1854* (Oxford: Oxford University Press, 1990), 353.

3. Joel H. Silbey, *Storm Over Texas: The Annexation Controversy and the Road to Civil War* (Oxford: Oxford University Press, 2005), xvii.

4. Randolph Campbell, *An Empire for Slavery: The Peculiar Institution in Texas, 1821–1865* (Baton Rouge, LA: Louisiana State University Press, 1989), 49.

5. Andrew J. Torget, *Seeds of Empire: Cotton, Slavery, and the Transformation of the Texas Borderlands, 1800–1850* (Chapel Hill, NC: University of North Carolina Press, 2015), 260–263.

6. For examples see Douglass' speeches on "The Kansas-Nebraska Bill," "The *Dred Scott* Decision," "The Slaveholder's Rebellion," and "The Blessings of Liberty and Education," in Frederick Douglass, *The Essential Douglass: Selected Writings and Speeches*, ed. Nicholas Buccola (Indianapolis, IN: Hackett Publishing, 2016), 107, 122, 170, 359.

7. Ulysses S. Grant, *Personal Memoirs of U. S. Grant and Selected Letters, 1839–*

1865, ed. Mary D. Feely and William S. Freely (New York: Library of America, 1990), 41–42.

8. See in particular Robert Seager II, *And Tyler Too: A Biography of John & Julia Gardiner Tyler* (New York: McGraw Hill, 1963); Edward P. Crapol, *John Tyler: The Accidental President* (Chapel Hill, NC: University of North Carolina Press, 2006); Christopher J. Leahy, *President Without a Party: The Life of John Tyler* (Baton Rouge, LA: Louisiana State University Press, 2020); Dan Monroe, *The Republican Vision of John Tyler* (College Station, TX: Texas A&M University Press, 2003); Norma Lois Peterson, *The Presidencies of William Henry Harrison and John Tyler* (Lawrence, KS: University Press of Kansas, 1989).

9. David A. Crockett, *The Oppositional Presidency: Leadership and the Constraints of History* (College Station, TX: Texas A&M University Press, 2002), 66.

10. For examples of this scholarly reassessment see Richard M. Pious, *The American Presidency* (New York: Basic Books, 1979), 62; Michael J. Gerhardt, *The Forgotten Presidents: Their Untold Constitutional Legacy* (Oxford: Oxford University Press, 2013), 38; Jordan T. Cash, "The Isolated Presidency: John Tyler and Unilateral Presidential Power," *American Political Thought* 7, no. 4 (Winter 2018): 47–49; Jordan T. Cash, *The Isolated Presidency* (Oxford: Oxford University Press, 2023).

11. Robert J. Spitzer, "John Tyler," in *The Presidents and the Constitution: A Living History*, ed. Ken Gormley (New York: New York University Press, 2016), 146, 137.

12. For examples of this literature see Scott Mainwaring and Matthew Shugart, *Presidentialism, and Democracy in Latin America* (Cambridge: Cambridge University Press, 1997); Alejandro Bonvecchi and Carlos Scartascini, "The Organization of the Executive Branch in Latin America: What We Know and What We Need to Know," *Latin American Politics and Society* 56, no. 1 (Spring 2014): 144–165; Javier Corrales, "Presidents, Ruling Parties, and Party Rules: A Theory on the Politics of Economic Reform in Latin America," *Comparative Politics* 32, no. 2 (Jan. 2000): 127–149; Jenny S. Martinez, "Inherent Executive Power: A Comparative Perspective," *Yale Law Journal* 115, no. 9 (2006): 2480–2511.

CHAPTER 1. THE TEX-MEX EXECUTIVE

1. Paul D. Lack, *The Texas Revolutionary Experience: A Political and Social History, 1835–1836* (College Station, TX: Texas A&M University Press, 1992), 88.

2. Clarence R. Wharton, *History of Texas* (Dallas: Turner, 1935), 132–133.

3. Wharton, *History of Texas*, 137.

4. Lack, *Texas Revolutionary Experience*, 84.

5. Lack, *Texas Revolutionary Experience*, 87–88; Rupert N. Richardson, "Framing the Constitution of the Republic of Texas," *Southwestern Historical Quarterly* 31, no. 3 (1928): 195. The delegates with previous experience in American politics were Robert Potter, Martin Palmer, Samuel P. Carson, and convention president Richard Ellis. Ellis, Palmer, and Carson were also the delegates who had experi-

ence drafting state constitutions. Houston attended the convention and was initially appointed to the committee to draft the constitution on March 3, but he was then appointed commander in chief on March 4 and left the convention on March 6, well before the constitution was completed. See H. P. N. Gammel, comp., *The Laws of Texas, 1822-1897* (Austin, TX: Gammel, 1898), 1:839, 1:847; Wharton, *History of Texas*, 133.

6. The other instances are the founding of Liberia in 1847 by free African Americans, the secession of the Southern states to form the Confederacy in 1861, and the short-lived Republic of Hawaii in 1894. For a discussion of the Liberian constitution in comparison to the American, see Jordan T. Cash, "'A Purer Form of Government': African American Constitutionalism in the Founding of Liberia," *Journal of Transatlantic Studies* 19, no. 4 (Dec. 2021): 408-440. For discussions of the Confederate constitution see Alison L. LaCroix, "Continuity in Secession: The Case of the Confederate Constitution," in *Nullification and Secession in Modern Constitutional Thought*, ed. Sanford Levinson (Lawrence, KS: University Press of Kansas, 2016), 274-293; James R. Stoner Jr., "The Case of the Confederate Constitution," in *The Political Thought of the Civil War*, ed. Alan Levine, Thomas W. Merrill, and James R. Stoner Jr. (Lawrence, KS: University Press of Kansas, 2018), 273-289.

7. Lack, *Texas Revolutionary Experience*, 84; James E. Crisp, "José Antonio Navarro: The Problem of Tejano Powerlessness," in *Tejano Leadership in Mexican and Revolutionary Texas*, ed. Jesús F. de la Teja (College Station, TX: Texas A&M University Press, 2010), 153; Margaret Swett Henson, *Lorenzo de Zavala: The Pragmatic Idealist* (Fort Worth, TX: Texas Christian University Press, 1996), 21-40, 59-70. For a unique insight into Zavala's perception of the United States, see Lorenzo de Zavala, *Journey to the United States of North America*, trans. Wallace Woolsey (Houston: Arte Público, 2005).

8. Daniel Walker Howe, *What Hath God Wrought: The Transformation of America, 1815-1848* (Oxford: Oxford University Press, 2007), 660; Crisp, "José Antonio Navarro," 153. The Texas Declaration of Independence refers several times to the Mexican constitution of 1824, asserting that the Mexican government "induced the Anglo American [sic] population of Texas to colonize its wilderness under the pledged faith of a written constitution" and charging Santa Anna with "having overturned the constitution of his country." See Texas, "Declaration of Independence."

9. Alexis de Tocqueville, *Democracy in America*, trans. Harvey C. Mansfield and Delba Winthrop (Chicago: University of Chicago Press, 2000), 156. I am grateful to Hance Winingham for reminding me of this passage.

10. Lack, *Texas Revolutionary Experience*, 89.

11. Jaime E. Rodríguez Ordóñez, "Constitution of 1824 and the Mexican State," in *The Origins of Mexican National Politics, 1808-1847*, ed. Jaime E. Rodriguez Ordóñez. (Wilmington, DE: Scholarly Resources, 1997), 83. See also Stanley C. Green, *The Mexican Republic: The First Decade, 1823-1832* (Pittsburgh, PA: University of Pittsburgh Press, 1987), 45.

12. Henry Clay to the editors of the Washington *Daily National Intelligencer*

[Joseph Gales and William W. Seaton], April 17, 1844, in *The Papers of Henry Clay*, ed. Robert Seager II and Melba Porter Hay (Lexington, KY: University Press of Kentucky, 1988), 10:46.

13. Stanley Siegel, *A Political History of the Texas Republic, 1836–1845* (Austin, TX: University of Texas Press, 1956), 14.

14. For the records we do have, see "Journals of the Convention of the Free, Sovereign, and Independent People of Texas, in General Convention, Assembled," in *TLT*, 1:821–904.

15. U.S. Const., art. II, sec. 4. The Texas constitution differs slightly in replacing "or" with "and" so the provision reads "treason, bribery, and other high crimes and misdemeanors." See Texas Const. (1836), art. VI, sec. 16.

16. Texas Const. (1836), art. III, Sec. 2; Mexico Const. (1824), title IV, sec. 1, art. 77; Coahuila y Tejas Const. (1827), title II, sec. 1, art. 112; "The Proposed Constitution for the State of Texas," in *Documents of Texas History*, ed. Ernest Wallace, David M. Vigness, and George B. Ward (Austin, TX: State House Press, 1994), 83; Alabama Const. (1819), art. IV, sec. 4; Tennessee Const. (1834) art. 3, sec. 4.

17. Texas Const. (1836), art. I, secs. 3 and 8. The terms for the Mexican Chamber of Deputies and the Senate were two- and four-years, respectively. See Mexico Const. (1824), title III, sec. 2, art. 8; Mexico Const. (1824), title III, sec. 3, art. 25. Even the unicameral legislature of Coahuila y Tejas had two-year terms for its deputies. See Coahuila y Tejas Const. (1827), title I, sec. 1, art. 44. The proposed 1833 constitution also had two-year terms for all members of its bicameral legislature. See "Proposed Constitution," in *DTH*, 83.

18. For a general description of the Anti-Federalists on this point see Herbert J. Storing, *What the Anti-Federalists Were For: The Political Thought of the Opponents of the Constitution* (Chicago: University of Chicago Press, 1981), 17.

19. The Twenty-second Amendment limiting American presidents to two terms would only be ratified in 1951. See U.S. Const., 22nd Amend.

20. Mexico Const. (1824), title IV, sec. 1, art. 77; Coahuila y Tejas Const. (1827), title II, sec. 1, art. 112.

21. Similar provisions concerning rotations in office were also present in the American state constitutions that Texas delegates had contributed to. See Alabama Const. (1819), art. IV, sec. 4; Tennessee Const. (1834) art. 3, sec. 4.

22. U.S. Const. art. II, sec. 2.

23. U.S. Const. art. I, Sec. 8; Alexander Hamilton, "Federalist 24," in Alexander Hamilton, James Madison, and John Jay, *The Federalist*, ed. J.R. Pole (Indianapolis, IN: Hackett, 2005), 128–129; Hamilton, "Federalist 69," in *The Federalist*, 369.

24. Joseph J. Ellis, *His Excellency: George Washington* (New York: Alfred A. Knopf, 2004), 225.

25. Mexico Const. (1824), title IV, sec. 4, art. 112; Coahuila y Tejas Const. (1827), title II, sec. 1, art. 113.

26. These instances are also laid out in the proposed 1833 constitution. See "Proposed Constitution," in *DTH*, 83; Texas Const. (1836), art. VI, secs. 4,14; U.S. Const. art. II, sec. 1.

27. Jordan T. Cash, "George Mason and the Ambiguity of Executive Power," *Presidential Studies Quarterly* 48, no. 4 (December 2018): 759.

28. Mexico Const. (1824), title V, sec. 2; Coahuila y Tejas Const. (1827), title III, Sec. 2; Texas Const. (1836), art. IV, sec. 9.

29. For examples see Alabama Const. (1819), art. V, sec. 12; North Carolina Const. (1835), art. XIII; Tennessee Const. (1834) art. 6, sec. 3.

30. For a sampling of the literature on the effect that American presidents can have on the courts, see Robert A. Dahl, "Decision-Making in Democracy: Supreme Court as National Policy-Maker," *Journal of Public Law* 6 (Spring 1957): 279–295; Jeffrey A. Segal, Richard J. Timpone and Robert M. Howard, "Buyer Beware? Presidential Success through Supreme Court Appointments," *Political Research Quarterly* 53, no. 3 (Sept. 2000): 557–573; David Cottrell, Charles R. Shipan, and Richard J. Anderson, "The Power to Appoint: Presidential Nominations and Change on the Supreme Court," *Journal of Politics* 81, no. 3 (July 2019): 1057–1068; Jack M. Balkin and Sanford Levinson, "Understanding the Constitutional Revolution," *Virginia Law Review* 87, no. 6 (Oct. 2001): 1045–1104.

31. U.S. Const. art. II, sec. 1; Mexico Const. (1824), title IV, sec. 1.

32. Texas Const. (1836) art. I, sec. 7; art. III, sec. 2; art. IV, sec. 14.

33. Coahuila y Tejas Const. (1827), Preamble and Preliminary Provisions; art. 31.

34. See Virginia Const. (1830), art. IV, sec. 1; South Carolina Const. (1790), art. II, sec. 1.

35. U.S. Const. Twelfth Amend.; Texas Const. (1836), art. VI, sec. 14.

36. Andrew Jackson, "First Annual Message to Congress, December 1829," https://millercenter.org/the-presidency/presidential-speeches/december-8-1829-first-annual-message-congress.

37. For an overview of other reform efforts into the twenty-first century see Jeremy D. Bailey, *The Idea of Presidential Representation: An Intellectual and Political History* (Lawrence, KS: University Press of Kansas, 2019), 42–81.

38. For a recent example of the removal power being debated in the courts see *Seila Law LLC v. Consumer Financial Protection Bureau*, 591 U.S. (2020).

39. Hamilton, "Federalist 77," in *Federalist*, 407.

40. *Annals of Congress*, House of Representatives, 1st Congress, 1st Session, 518. For further discussions of Hamilton's and Madison's views on the removal power see Jeremy D. Bailey, "The New Unitary Executive and Democratic Theory: The Problem of Alexander Hamilton," *American Political Science Review* 102, no. 4 (Nov. 2008): 453–465; Jeremy D. Bailey, *James Madison and Constitutional Imperfection* (Cambridge: Cambridge University Press, 2015), 61–69.

41. William S. Stokes, "Whig Conceptions of Executive Power," *Presidential Studies Quarterly* 6, no. ½ (Winter-Spring 1976), 17.

42. *Register of Debates*, Senate, 23rd Session, 1st Session, 66, 834–836. For a detailed examination of the removal power debate from the founding to the twenty-first century see J. David Alvis, Jeremy D. Bailey, and F. Flagg Taylor IV, *The Contested Removal Power, 1789–2010* (Lawrence: University Press of Kansas, 2013).

43. Mexico Const. (1824), title IV, sec. 4, art. 110. The term "secretaries of state" refers to all cabinet officials, not only the one who handles foreign affairs.

44. Coahuila y Tejas Const. (1827), title II, sec. 1, art. 113.

45. Rodríguez Ordóñez, "Constitution of 1834," 83; Mexico Const. (1824), title IV, secs. 5–6.

46. Coahuila y Tejas Const. (1827), title II, secs. 4–6.

47. "Proposed Constitution," in *DTH*, 83; James Madison, *Notes of Debates in the Federal Convention of 1787* (New York: W. W. Norton, 1987), 472; Jeffrey S. Sutton, *Who Decides?: States as Laboratories of Constitutional Experimentation* (Oxford: Oxford University Press, 2021), 147–182; Cash, "Mason," 757.

48. Notably, the first act of the Texas Congress was to create the offices of secretary of the treasury, war, and the navy, as well as those of the attorney general and postmaster general, the same configuration as the American cabinet at the time. See "Laws of the Republic of Texas," in *TLT*, 1:1087.

49. Texas Const. (1836), art. VI, sec. 10.

50. Robert F. Williams, "Evolving State Legislative and Executive Power in the Founding Decade," *Annals of the American Academy of Political and Social Science* 496, no. 1 (1988): 43–53; Cash, "Mason," 741–767.

CHAPTER 2. HIS ACCIDENCY, JOHN TYLER

1. Christopher J. Leahy, *President Without a Party: The Life of John Tyler* (Baton Rouge, LA: Louisiana State University Press, 2020), 12; Lyon Gardiner Tyler, *The Letters and Times of the Tylers* (New York: Da Capo, 1970), 3:7.

2. Tyler, *Letters*, 3:5–6; Dan Monroe, *The Republican Vision of John Tyler* (College Station, TX: Texas A&M University Press, 2003), 13; Edward P. Crapol, *John Tyler: The Accidental President* (Chapel Hill, NC: University of North Carolina Press, 2006), 30–31. By strange coincidence, one of men who served in the House of Delegates with Madison, Marshall, and the elder Tyler was Benjamin Harrison, the father of the younger Tyler's future running mate.

3. Leahy, *President Without a Party*, 24.

4. Crapol, *John Tyler*, 36.

5. Tyler, *Letters*, 1:282. Notably, when Tyler left Congress in 1821, he endorsed Stevenson as his successor, and Stevenson went on to serve as Speaker of the United States House of Representatives from 1827–1834.

6. Jordan T. Cash, "The Court and the Old Dominion: Judicial Review Among the Virginia Jeffersonians," *Law and History Review* 35, no. 2 (May 2017): 356. See also Norman K. Risjord, *The Old Republicans: Southern Conservatism in the Age of Jefferson* (New York: Columbia University Press, 1965), 267–270.

7. Jeffrey L. Pasley, "Slavery, War, and Democracy: The Winding Road to the Missouri Crisis," in *A Fire Bell in the Past: The Missouri Crisis at 200*, ed. Jeffrey L. Pasley and John Craig Hammond (Columbia: University of Missouri Press, 2021), 113–157; Daniel Walker Howe, *What Hath God Wrought: The Transformation of America, 1815–1848* (Oxford: Oxford University Press, 2007), 147; William

W. Freehling, *The Road to Disunion: Secessionists at Bay, 1776–1854* (Oxford: Oxford University Press, 1990), 144; Sean Wilentz, "Jeffersonian Democracy and the Origins of Political Antislavery in the United States: The Missouri Crisis Revisited," *Journal of the Historical Society* 4, no. 3 (Fall 2004): 377–395. For an overview of the constitutional issues raised during the congressional debate over the Missouri Compromise see the essays in William S. Belko, ed., *Contesting the Constitution: Congress Debates the Missouri Crisis, 1819–1821* (Columbia: University of Missouri Press, 2021).

8. Monroe, *Republican Vision of John Tyler*, 40.
9. *Annals of Congress*, House of Representatives, 16th Congress, 1st Session, 1383.
10. *Annals of Congress*, House of Representatives, 16th Congress, 1st Session, 1383.
11. *Annals of Congress*, House of Representatives, 16th Congress, 1st Session, 1389.
12. *Annals of Congress*, House of Representatives, 16th Congress, 1st Session, 1387.
13. *Annals of Congress*, House of Representatives, 16th Congress, 1st Session, 1389.
14. Leahy, *President Without a Party*, 61.
15. For Jefferson's support of diffusion see Jefferson to John Holmes, April 22, 1820. https://founders.archives.gov/documents/Jefferson/03-15-02-0518; Jefferson to Marquis de Lafayette, December 26, 1820, https://founders.archives.gov/documents/Jefferson/98-01-02-1708. For Madison's support of diffusion see Madison to Robert Walsh, Jr., November 27, 1819, https://founders.archives.gov/documents/Madison/04-01-02-0504.
16. *Annals of Congress*, House of Representatives, 16th Congress, 1st Session, 1392–1393. For discussion on Tyler's support of diffusion see Monroe, *Republican Vision of John Tyler*, 43; Crapol. *John Tyler*, 38; Freehling, *Road to Disunion*, 151; Leahy, *President Without a Party*, 62.
17. Crapol, *John Tyler*, 39. For a description of the "national greatness" ideology and its relationship to other foreign policy ideologies see Michael H. Hunt, *Ideology and U.S. Foreign Policy* (New Haven, CT: Yale University Press, 2009).
18. Howe, *What Hath God*, 152.
19. Tyler, *Letters*, 1:324.
20. Oliver Chitwood, *John Tyler: Champion of the Old South* (New York: Russell and Russell, 1964), 63.
21. For the full speech see Tyler, *Letters*, 1:346–354.
22. Chitwood, *John Tyler*, 80; Risjord, *Old Republicans*, 267–268; Leahy, *President Without a Party*, 72–76; Robert Seager II, *And Tyler Too: A Biography of John & Julia Gardiner Tyler* (New York: McGraw Hill, 1963), 29; Tyler, *Letters* 1:256.
23. Tyler, *Letters*, 436; Crapol, *John Tyler*, 42.
24. For recent historical surveys on the election of 1824 see Donald Ratcliffe, *The One-Party Presidential Contest: Adams, Jackson, and 1824's Five-Horse Race* (Lawrence, KS: University Press of Kansas, 2015); Sean Wilentz, *The Rise of American Democracy: Jefferson to Lincoln* (New York: W. W. Norton, 2005), 240–257; Howe, *What Hath God*, 203–211.
25. John Quincy Adams, *Memoirs of John Quincy Adams: Comprising Portions of his Diary from 1795 to 1848*, ed. Charles Francis Adams (Philadelphia: J. B.

Lippincott, 1876), 6:474. For a discussion of Adams' non-partisanship see Daniel Walker Howe, *The Political Culture of the American Whigs* (Chicago: The University of Chicago Press, 1979), 49–52; Mary W. M. Hargreaves, *The Presidency of John Quincy Adams* (Lawrence, KS: University Press of Kansas, 1985), 66.

26. Robert V. Remini, *Martin Van Buren and the Making of the Democratic Party* (New York: Columbia University Press, 1959), 123–185; James W. Ceaser, *Presidential Selection: Theory and Development* (Princeton: Princeton University Press, 1979), 125–131; John H. Aldrich, *Why Parties?: The Origin and Transformation of Political Parties in America* (Chicago: University of Chicago Press, 1995), 97–100.

27. Tyler, *Letters*, 1:377.

28. *Annals of Congress*, 15th Congress, 2nd Session, 925–935; Monroe, *Republican Vision of John Tyler*, 34–38.

29. Leahy, *President Without a Party*, 68.

30. Tyler, *Letters*, 1:360.

31. Tyler, 1:372.

32. Tyler, 1:386.

33. Seager, *And Tyler Too*, 89.

34. Monroe, *Republican Vision of John Tyler*, 150; Seager, *And Tyler Too*, 84.

35. Tyler, *Letters*, 1:429

36. For a full account of the Nullification Crisis see Richard E. Ellis, *The Union at Risk: Jacksonian Democracy, States' Rights, and the Nullification Crisis* (Oxford: Oxford University Press, 1987). See also Donald B. Cole, *The Presidency of Andrew Jackson* (Lawrence, KS: University Press of Kansas, 1993), 158–180. For South Carolina's full argument for nullification, see John C. Calhoun, "Exposition and Protest," in *Union and Liberty: The Political Philosophy of John C. Calhoun*, ed. Ross M. Lence (Indianapolis: Liberty Fund, 1992), 311–365. For Jackson's response see Andrew Jackson, "Nullification Proclamation," December 10, 1832, https://miller center.org/the-presidency/presidential-speeches/december-10-1832-nullifica tion-proclamation.

37. *Register of Debates*, Senate, 22nd Congress, 2nd Session, 359–374.

38. For a full description of this event see Cole, *Presidency of Andrew Jackson*, 186–200.

39. *Register of Debates*, Senate, 23rd Congress, 1st Session, 663–676.

40. Tyler, *Letters*, 1:490–491.

41. *Register of Debates*, Senate, 23rd Congress, 1st Session, 677–679.

42. Arthur Charles Cole, *The Whig Party in the South* (Gloucester, MA: American Historical Association, 1962), 29–30.

43. U.S. Const. Art. I, Sec. 5.

44. Chitwood, *John Tyler*, 27–28; Gary May, *John Tyler* (New York: Henry Holt, 2008), 45–46.

45. Michael F. Holt, *The Rise and Fall of the American Whig Party: Jacksonian Politics and the Onset of the Civil War* (Oxford: Oxford University Press, 1999), 38–45; Howe, *What Hath God*, 478.

46. Richard J. Ellis, *Old Tip vs. The Sly Fox: The 1840 Election and the Making of a Partisan Nation* (Lawrence, KS: University Press of Kansas, 2020), 152.

47. John Tyler to Henry Clay, September 18, 1839, in *The Papers of Henry Clay*, ed. Robert Seager II and Melba Porter Hay (Lexington, KY: The University Press of Kentucky, 1988), 9:342.

48. David S. Heidler and Jeanne T. Heidler, *Henry Clay: The Essential American* (New York: Random House, 2010), 308.

49. "Harrisburg Convention, December 11, 1841," in *Niles National Register, From September, 1841, to March, 1842* 61, ed. Jeremiah Hughes (Baltimore: Exchange Place, 1842), 232. See also Leahy, *President Without a Party*, 1-2, Ellis, *Old Tip vs. The Sly Fox*, 150.

50. Norma Lois Peterson, *The Presidencies of William Henry Harrison and John Tyler* (Lawrence, KS: University Press of Kansas, 1989), 29.

51. Peterson, *Presidencies*, 41.

52. U.S. Const., Art. II, Sec. 1.

53. Jordan T. Cash, "The Isolated Presidency: John Tyler and Unilateral Presidential Power," *American Political Thought* 7, no. 4 (Winter 2018): 35.

54. Cash, "Isolated Presidency," 34.

55. William Cranch, "Oath of Office Administered to President John Tyler in the Presence of the Cabinet," in James Daniel Richardson, comp., *The Compilation of the Messages and Papers of the Presidents*, (New York: Bureau of National Literature, 1909), 4:1886.

56. Crapol, *John Tyler*, 13; Cash, "Isolated Presidency," 34.

57. U.S. Const. Amend. XXV, Sec. 1; Jordan T. Cash, "The Constitutional Agency of the Vice Presidency," *Congress & the Presidency* 49, no. 1 (2022): 1-34. For more on the Twenty-Fifth Amendment see John D. Feerick, *The Twenty-Fifth Amendment: Its Complete History and Applications* (New York: Fordham University Press, 2014).

58. Adams, *Memoirs*, 10:463.

59. For examples see Clay's letters to James F. Conover, April 9, 1841; John L. Lawrence, April 13, 1841; John M. Berrien, April 20, 1841; Richard Hines and the Wake County Whigs, March 21, 1842; John M. Berrien, December 9, 1843, in *PHC*, 9:519, 9:521, 9:681, 9:900.

60. John Tyler, "Inaugural Message," in Richardson, 4:1890.

61. Leonard Dinnerstein, "The Accession of John Tyler to the Presidency," *Virginia Magazine of History and Biography* 70, no. 4 (Oct. 1962): 450-453; Robert J. Morgan, *A Whig Embattled: The Presidency Under John Tyler* (Lincoln, NE: University of Nebraska Press, 1954), 12-18.

62. Michael J. Gerhardt, "Constitutional Construction and Departmentalism: A Case Study of the Demise of the Whig Presidency" *University of Pennsylvania Journal of Constitutional Law* 12, no. 2 (Apr. 2010): 437.

63. John Alexander Tyler interview with Frank G. Carpenter, "A Talk with a President's Son," *Lippincott's Monthly Magazine* 41 (March 1888), 416-417. See also Leonard D. White, *The Jacksonians: A Study in Administrative History, 1829-1861* (New York: Macmillan, 1954), 86; Peterson, *Presidencies of William Henry Harrison and John Tyler*, 52.

64. John Tyler, "Inaugural Message," in Richardson, 4:1891-1892.

65. John Tyler, "Special Session Message," in Richardson, 4:1893–1904; Morgan, *A Whig Embattled*, 19. For an analysis of Tyler's general rhetoric see David Zarefsky, "John Tyler and the Rhetoric of the Accidental Presidency" in *Before the Rhetorical Presidency*, ed. Martin J. Medhurst (College Station, TX: Texas A&M University Press, 2008), 66.

66. Clay to James F. Conover, April 9, 1841, in *PHC*, 9:518.

67. John Tyler, "Veto Messages," in Richardson, 4:1919–1920.

68. Holt, *Whig Party*, 137.

69. "Congressional Whig Meeting, September 13, 1841," in *Niles National Register*, 35–36; Seager, *And Tyler Too*, 160–162; May, *John Tyler*, 75–77.

70. Cash, "Isolated Presidency," 28.

71. Tyler, *Letters*, 2:128.

72. Tyler, "Special Session Message," in Richardson, 4:1895.

73. Tyler, *Letters*, 2:254.

CHAPTER 3. SAM HOUSTON AND THE REPUBLIC OF TEXAS

1. David J. Weber, *The Spanish Frontier in North America* (New Haven, CT: Yale University Press, 2009), 213. See also Philip Coolidge Brooks, *Diplomacy and the Borderlands: The Adams-Onís Treaty of 1819* (New York: Octagon Books, 1970), 40.

2. Brooks, *Diplomacy and the Borderlands*, 163; Richard Bruce Winders, *Crisis in the Southwest: The United States, Mexico, and the Struggle over Texas* (Wilmington, DE: SR Books, 2002), 3; Jon Kukla, *A Wilderness So Immense: The Louisiana Purchase and the Destiny of America* (New York: Alfred A. Knopf, 2003), 331–332.

3. Thomas Jefferson to James Monroe, May 14, 1820, https://founders.archives.gov/documents/Jefferson/03-15-02-0555.

4. Buckner F. Melton, Jr., *Aaron Burr: Conspiracy to Treason* (New York: John Wiley and Sons, 2002), 232.

5. James M. McPherson, *Battle Cry of Freedom: The Civil War Era* (Oxford: Oxford University Press, 2003), 105.

6. Robert E. May, *Manifest Destiny's Underworld: Filibustering in Antebellum America* (Chapel Hill: University of North Carolina Press, 2004), xii.

7. Winders, *Crisis in the Southwest*, 74–75.

8. Winders, *Crisis*, 76; Ed Bradley, "Fighting for Texas: Filibuster James Long, the Adams-Onís Treaty, and the Monroe Administration," *Southwestern Historical Quarterly* 102, no. 3 (Jan. 1999): 326–328.

9. Mexican Const., Title II, Sec. 1; Barbara A. Tenenbaum, "The Making of a Fait Accompli: Mexico and the Provincias Internas, 1776–1846," in *The Origins of Mexican National Politics, 1808–1847*, ed. Jaime E. Rodriguez Ordóñez. (Wilmington, DE: Scholarly Resources, 1997), 92.

10. Frederick Merk, *History of the Westward Movement* (New York: Alfred A. Knopf, 1978), 267.

11. For an overview of Austin's life and work, especially as an *empresario*, see

Gregg Centrell, *Stephen F. Austin: Empresario of Texas* (Austin, TX: Texas State Historical Association, 2016), 63–171.

12. Joel H. Silbey, *Storm Over Texas: The Annexation Controversy and the Road to Civil War* (Oxford: Oxford University Press, 2005), 7.

13. Daniel Walker Howe, *What Hath God Wrought: The Transformation of America, 1815–1848* (Oxford: Oxford University Press, 2007), 659.

14. Mary W. M. Hargreaves, *The Presidency of John Quincy Adams* (Lawrence, KS: University Press of Kansas, 1985), 55; Howe, *What Hath God*, 258.

15. Timothy J. Henderson, *A Glorious Defeat: Mexico and Its War with the United States* (New York: Hill and Wang, 2007), 42–43. See also Adams's brief comment approving the offer in John Quincy Adams, *Memoirs of John Quincy Adams: Comprising Portions of his Diary from 1795 to 1848*, ed. Charles Francis Adams (Philadelphia: J. B. Lippincott, 1876), 7:240.

16. Treaty of Limits, January 28, 1828, https://texashistory.unt.edu/ark:/67531/metapth31220/.

17. Andrew Jackson to Martin Van Buren, August 12, 1829, in *The Correspondence of Andrew Jackson*, ed. John Spencer Bassett (Washington, D.C.: Carnegie Institution of Washington, 1929), 4:57.

18. Donald B. Cole, *The Presidency of Andrew Jackson* (Lawrence, KS: University Press of Kansas, 1993), 130–133.

19. James Haley, *Sam Houston* (Norman, OK: University of Oklahoma Press, 2002), 4–6.

20. Haley, *Sam Houston*, 9–10; Jack Gregory and Rennard Strickland, *Sam Houston with the Cherokees, 1829–1833* (Norman, OK: University of Oklahoma Press, 1995), 9.

21. Marquis James, *The Raven: A Biography of Sam Houston* (New York: Blue Ribbon, 1929), 20; Haley, *Sam Houston*, 9.

22. Haley, *Sam Houston*, 34–35.

23. *Annals of Congress*, House of Representatives, 18th Congress, 1st Session, 1161.

24. For a broader discussion of that debate see Jordan T. Cash, "'The Voice of America': The Speaker of the House and Foreign Policy Agenda-Setting," *Polity* 53, no. 4 (October 2021): 673–675.

25. *Annals of Congress*, House of Representatives, 18th Congress, 1st Session, 1162.

26. *Annals of Congress*, House of Representatives, 18th Congress, 1st Session, 1162; Cash, "Voice of America," 675.

27. Sam Houston to Captain W. V. Cobbs, February 7, 1825 in *The Writings of Sam Houston, 1813–1863*, ed. Amelia W. Williams and Eugene C. Barker (Austin, TX: University of Texas Press, 1939), 2:9.

28. "Extract from a Circular of Mr. Houston to the Freemen of the Ninth Congressional District of the State of Tennessee, dated Washington, D.C., March 3, 1825," in William Carey Crane, *Life and Select Literary Remains of Sam Houston of Texas* (Dallas: William G. Scarff, 1884), 180.

29. Haley, *Sam Houston*, 44.

30. Gregory and Strickland, *Sam Houston with the Cherokees*, 3.

31. For a full discussion of the marriage see Elizabeth Cook, "Sam Houston and Eliza Allen: The Marriage and the Mystery," *Southwestern Historical Quarterly* 94, no. 1 (Jul. 1990): 1-36.

32. Specifically, Mexico granted Texas another representative in the Coahuila y Tejas state legislature, introduced trial by jury, and recognized English as a second official language in the state. See William C. Davis, *Lone Star Rising: The Revolutionary Birth of the Texas Republic* (College Station, TX: Texas A&M University Press, 2006), 117; Will Fowler, *Santa Anna of Mexico* (Lincoln, NE: University of Nebraska Press, 2007), 145.

33. Michael P. Costeloe, *The Central Republic in Mexico, 1835-1846: 'Hombres de Bien' in the Age of Santa Anna* (Cambridge: Cambridge University Press, 2002), 93-101.

34. Fowler, *Santa Anna*, 162.

35. James, *The Raven*, 214; Haley, *Sam Houston*, 116.

36. Howe, *What Hath God*, 661.

37. Davis, *Lone Star Rising*, 161-173

38. "Journals of the Convention of 1836," in *The Papers of the Texas Revolution, 1835-1836* (Austin, TX: Presidial, 1973), 9:303.

39. "Journals of the Convention of 1836," in *The Papers of the Texas Revolution, 1835-1836*, 9:310.

40. For a full description of Santa Anna's life and career, becoming the dominant figure in Mexican politics from independence to the 1850s, see Fowler, *Santa Anna*.

41. William C. Binkley, *The Texas Revolution* (Baton Rouge, LA: Louisiana State University Press, 1979), 107-108; Davis, *Lone Star Rising*, 242-246; Haley, *Sam Houston*, 128-142.

42. Davis, *Lone Star Rising*, 266-272; Brinkley, *The Texas Revolution*, 108-109; Haley, 147-151; Stephen L. Harden, *Texian Iliad: A Military History of the Texas Revolution* (Austin, TX: University of Texas Press, 1996), 213.

43. Howe, *What Hath God*, 667-669. For the full text of the treaty see "The Treaty of Velasco," in *Documents of Texas History*, ed. Ernest Wallace, David M. Vigness, and George B. Ward (Austin, TX: State House Press, 1994), 117-118.

44. Stanley Siegel, *A Political History of the Texas Republic, 1836-1845* (Austin, TX: University of Texas Press, 1956), 47.

45. Siegel, *Texas Republic*, 50.

46. Davis, *Lone Star Rising*, 299.

47. Sam Houston, "President Houston's First Inaugural Address," in *DTH*, 124.

48. Sam Houston to John H. Houston, November 20, 1836, in *WSH*, 2:27.

49. Robert V. Remini, *Andrew Jackson: The Course of American Democracy, 1833-1845* (Baltimore: John Hopkins University Press, 1998), 3:352.

50. Benjamin Lundy, *The War in Texas* (Philadelphia, 1836), 3.

51. Cole, *Presidency of Andrew Jackson*, 266.

52. Jackson to Santa Anna, September 4, 1836, printed in *Register of Debates*, Senate, 24th Congress, 2nd Session, 256.

53. Andrew Jackson, "Special Message," December 21, 1836, https://www.presidency.ucsb.edu/documents/special-message-4009.

54. Sam Houston to Thomas Toby, January 27, 1837, in *WSH*, 2:41.

55. Foweler, *Santa Anna*, 183; James, *The Raven*, 275.

56. *Register of Debates*, House of Representatives, 24th Congress, 2nd Session, 1880-1881.

57. *Register of Debates*, Senate, 24th Congress, 2nd Session, 1013.

58. Andrew Jackson, "Special Message," March 3, 1837, https://www.presidency.ucsb.edu/documents/special-message-3205; Cole, *Presidency of Andrew Jackson*, 267; James, *The Raven*, 275-276.

59. Major L. Wilson, *The Presidency of Martin Van Buren* (Lawrence, KS: University Press of Kansas, 1984), 18.

60. John Forsyth to Memucan Hunt, August 25, 1837, in *House Executive Documents* 40, 25th Congress, 1st Session no. 311, 2-18; Wilson, *Presidency of Martin Van Buren*, 151.

61. Forsyth to Hunt, August 25, 1837, in *House Executive Documents* 40, 25th Congress, 1st Session no. 311, 2-18.

62. Martin Van Buren to Thomas Ritchie, January 13, 1827, http://vanburenpapers.org/document-mvb00528.

63. Wilson, *Presidency of Martin Van Buren*, 149-152; Jeffrey Rogers Hummel, "Martin Van Buren: The American Gladstone," in *Reassessing the Presidency: The Rise of the Executive State and the Decline of Freedom*, ed. John V. Denson (Auburn, AL: Ludwig von Mises Institute, 2001), 173.

64. Peter W. Grayson to Robert Anderson Irion, December 7, 1837, in *Diplomatic Correspondence of the Republic of Texas*, ed. George Garrison (Washington, D.C.: Government Printing Office, 1908), 2:273.

65. Memucan Hunt to the Texian Legation, September 18, 1837, in *DCRT*, 2:1:259.

66. For an in-depth discussion of this switch see R. R. Stenberg, "J. Q. Adams: Imperialist and Apostate," *Southwestern Social Science Quarterly* 16, no. 4 (Mar. 1936): 37-49.

67. Silbey, *Storm Over Texas*, 11-12; David M. Pletcher, *The Diplomacy of Annexation: Texas, Oregon, and the Mexican War* (Columbia, MO: University of Missouri Press, 1973), 57. For the record of Adams's speeches see the days from June 16 to July 7, 1838 in *Congressional Globe*, 25th Congress, 2nd Session.

68. *Journal of the House of Representatives of the Republic of Texas*, 2nd Congress, Adjourned Session, 32.

69. For examples see William Wharton to Stephen Austin, January 6, 1837; Hunt to Irion, August 4, 1837; Hunt to Irion, October 21, 1837; and Hunt to Irion, January 31, 1838, *DCRT*, 2:169-170; 2:1: 246; 2:266-267; 2:284-285.

70. Hunt to Irion, January 31, 1838, in *DCRT*, 2:284.

71. Joseph William Schmitz, *Texan Statecraft, 1836–1845* (San Antonio: Naylor Company, 1941), 62; Siegel, *Texas Republic*, 91.

72. Schmitz, *Texan Statecraft*, 64. See also Pletcher, *Diplomacy of Annexation*, 79; Siegel, *Texas Republic*, 87–88; Henderson to Irion, January 5, 1838 in *DCRT*, 2:839–842.

73. Siegel, *Texas Republic*, 89.

74. Schmitz, *Texan Statecraft*, 78; Siegel, *Texas Republic*, 91.

75. Haley, *Sam Houston*, 205.

76. Mirabeau Lamar, "Inaugural Address," December 10, 1838, in *DTH*, 126.

77. Lamar did, however, secure several commercial treaties with Britain, but these did not constitute formal recognition. Siegel, *Texas Republic*, 150; Stanley Siegel, *The Poet President of Texas: The Life of Mirabeau B. Lamar, President of the Republic of Texas* (Austin, TX: Jenkins, 1977), 77–78.

78. For an overview of Lamar's administration see Siegel, *Texas Republic*, 100–182.

79. Merk, *Westward*, 276.

80. Jackson's views were described in a letter from William H. Wharton to John Forsyth, January 24, 1837 in *DCRT*, 2:193–194.

81. Winder, *Crisis*, 50; Kenneth E. Hendrickson, *The Chief Executives of Texas: From Stephen F. Austin to John B. Connally, Jr.* (College Station, TX: Texas A&M University Press, 1995), 38–39.

82. Hendrickson, *The Chief Executives of Texas*, 39.

83. Houston to Anna Raguet, December 10, 1839, in *WSH*, 2:322.

84. Siegel, *Poet President*, 78.

85. Haley, *Sam Houston*, 217.

86. Haley, *Sam Houston*, 227.

87. Sam Houston, "First Message to Congress, Second Administration," in *WSH*, 2:400.

CHAPTER 4. THE ANNEXATION TREATY

1. Edward P. Crapol, *John Tyler: The Accidental President* (Chapel Hill, NC: University of North Carolina Press, 2006), 167–168; Jordan T. Cash, "The Isolated Presidency: John Tyler and Unilateral Presidential Power," *American Political Thought* 7, no. 4 (Winter 2018): 40.

2. Stanley Siegel, *A Political History of the Texas Republic, 1836–1845* (Austin, TX: University of Texas Press, 1956), viii.

3. Richard Bruce Winders, *Crisis in the Southwest: The United States, Mexico, and the Struggle over Texas* (Wilmington, DE: SR Books, 2002), 51; Siegel, *Texas Republic*, 192–193; Andrew J. Torget, *Seeds of Empire: Cotton, Slavery, and the Transformation of the Texas Borderlands, 1800–1850* (Chapel Hill, NC: University of North Carolina Press, 2015), 219.

4. Sam Houston, "A General Call to Arms," March 10, 1842, in *The Writings of Sam Houston, 1813–1863*, ed. Amelia W. Williams and Eugene C. Barker (Austin, TX: University of Texas Press, 1939), 2:490.

5. Sam Houston, "Message to the Texas Congress, June 27, 1842, in *WSH*, 3:74-78.
6. Siegel, *Texas Republic*, 197-198.
7. Siegel, *Texas Republic*, 199.
8. Stephen L. Harden, *Texian Iliad: A Military History of the Texas Revolution* (Austin, TX: University of Texas Press, 1996), 206.
9. Sam Houston, "Veto Message," July 22, 1842, in *WSH*, 3:114-124. Notably, Jackson wrote to Houston to praise his veto, telling his former protégé that "by your veto you have saved your country, and yourself from disgrace. *Stand on the Defensive*." See Jackson to Houston, August 17, 1842, in *WSH*, 3:125.
10. Houston to Alexander Somervell, October 3, 1842, in *WSH*, 3:170.
11. Winders, *Crisis in the Southwest*, 60-63; Siegel, *Texas Republic*, 205-208; James Haley, *Sam Houston* (Norman, OK: University of Oklahoma Press, 2002), 258-259.
12. Haley, *Sam Houston*, 236-237; Herbert Gambrell, *Anson Jones: The Last President of Texas* (Austin, TX: University of Texas Press, 1964), 213-219.
13. Siegel, *Texas Republic*, 185.
14. Wise's speech and Gilmer's letter are both reprinted in Frederick Merk, *Slavery and the Annexation of Texas* (New York: Alfred A. Knopf, 1972), 192-204. For John Quincy Adams's speech see John Quincy Adams, "To his constituents of the Twelfth Congressional District, at Braintree, 17th September, 1842," in *Niles National Register, From September 1842, to March 1843*, ed. Jeremiah Hughes (Baltimore, MD: Exchange Place, 1843), 138. See also Norma Lois Peterson, *The Presidencies of William Henry Harrison and John Tyler* (Lawrence, KS: University Press of Kansas, 1989), 176-177; Matthew Karp, *This Vast Southern Empire: Slaveholders at the Helm of American Foreign Policy* (Cambridge: Harvard University Press, 2016), 84.
15. John Tyler to Daniel Webster, October 11, 1841 in *The Papers of Daniel Webster*, ed. Harold D. Moser (Hanover, NH: University Press of New England, 1982), 5:167.
16. Daniel Webster, *The Diplomatic and Official Papers of Daniel Webster While Secretary of State* (New York: Harper and Brothers, 1848), 307.
17. Robert V. Remini, *Daniel Webster: The Man and His Time* (New York: W. W. Norton, 1997), 583.
18. Paul A. Varg, *Edward Everett: The Intellectual in the Turmoil of Politics* (Selinsgrove, PA: Susquehanna University Press, 1992), 116.
19. Claude H. Hall, *Abel Parker Upshur: Conservative Virginian 1790-1844* (Madison, WI: State Historical Society of Wisconsin, 1964), 31, 111.
20. Upshur quoted in Merk, *Slavery and Annexation*, 18; Peterson, *Presidencies of William Henry Harrison and John Tyler*, 178; Hall, *Abel Parker Upshur*, 196-197.
21. Reily quoted in Tyler, *Letters*, 2:256.
22. Peterson, *Presidencies of William Henry Harrison and John Tyler*, 177-178; Cash, "Isolated Presidency," 44.
23. Isaac Van Zandt to Anson Jones, March 13, 1843, in *Diplomatic Correspondence of the Republic of Texas*, ed. George Garrison (Washington, D.C.: Government Printing Office, 1908), 2:136-137.

24. Iwan Morgan, "French Policy in Spanish America: 1830–48," *Journal of Latin American Studies* 10, no. 2 (Nov. 1978): 309.

25. R. A. McLemore, "The Influence of French Diplomatic Policy on the Annexation of Texas," *Southwestern Historical Quarterly* 43, no. 3 (Jan.1940): 342. For a broader discussion of Guizot's foreign policy see Douglas Johnson, "The Foreign Policy of Guizot, 1840–1848," *University of Birmingham Historical Journal* 6 (1957–1958): 62–87.

26. Ashbel Smith to Anson Jones, June 3, 1842 in *DCRT*, 2:961.

27. David M. Pletcher, *The Diplomacy of Annexation: Texas, Oregon, and the Mexican War* (Columbia, MO: University of Missouri Press, 1973), 83.

28. Torget, *Seeds of Empire*, 221.

29. Haley, *Sam Houston*, 262–263.

30. Marquis James, *The Raven: A Biography of Sam Houston* (New York: Blue Ribbon, 1929), 343; J. L. Worley, "The Diplomatic Relations of England and the Republic of Texas," *Quarterly of the Texas State Historical Association* 9, no. 1 (July 1905): 14. For the text of the three treaties ratifying in the summer of 1842 see H. P. N. Gammel, comp., *The Laws of Texas, 1822–1897* (Austin, TX: Gammel, 1898), 2:880–904.

31. François Guizot and Lord Aberdeen quoted in Charles Elliot to Sam Houston, November 6, 1842. This letter was enclosed with another letter from Anson Jones to Isaac Van Zandt, December 25, 1842, in *DCRT*, 2:637. Haley, *Sam Houston*, 263.

32. William W. Freehling, *The Road to Disunion: Secessionists at Bay, 1776–1854* (Oxford: Oxford University Press, 1990), 370.

33. Sam Houston to Charles Elliot, May 13, 1843, in *British Diplomatic Correspondence Concerning the Republic of Texas, 1838–1846*, ed. Ephraim Douglass Adams (Austin, TX: Texas State Historical Association, 1917), 210–211.

34. Siegel, *Texas Republic*, 223; Freehling, *Road to Disunion*, 370–371; Haley, *Sam Houston*, 273–276.

35. Torget, *Seeds of Empire*, 237.

36. Ashbel Smith to Anson Jones, July 2, 1843, in *DCRT*, 2:1101. Interestingly, Smith reports that "a considerable party" in Britain envisioned Texas as "a refuge for fugitive slaves from the United States" which might act as "a sort of continental Hayti [sic], populated chiefly by blacks." Notably, Charles Elliot shared this vision, believing that such an outcome would create "a bound marked, beyond which Slavery could not advance." See Charles Elliot to Henry Unwin Addington, November 15, 1842, in *BDC-ROT*, 128. See also Torget, *Seeds of Empire*, 237–238.

37. Lord Abderdeen quoted in Ashbel Smith to Anson Jones, July 31, 1843 in *DCRT*, 2:1117.

38. Ashbel Smith to Isaac Van Zandt, January 25, 1843, in *DCRT*, 2:1105–1106. See also Smith's second letter to Van Zandt on January 25, 1843 which asserts that British financial support of Mexico was provided by British abolitionists, as well as his letter to Jones on July 3, 1843 which again emphasized the centrality of

slavery to further Anglo-Texian relations. For the former see 2:1108, for the latter 2:1108.

39. Ashbel Smith to Anson Jones, July 31, 1843, in *DCRT*, 2:1117.

40. Ashbel Smith to John C. Calhoun, June 19, 1843, in *The Papers of John C. Calhoun*, ed. Clyde N. Wilson and Shirley Bright Cook (Columbia, SC: University of South Carolina Press, 1987), 17:253.

41. Ashbel Smith to Isaac Van Zandt, January 25, 1843, in *DCRT*, 2:1103–1107.

42. Isaac Van Zandt to Anson Jones, March 13, 1843, in *DCRT*, 2:135; Freehling, *Road to Disunion*, 369.

43. Jesse S. Reeves, *American Diplomacy under Tyler and Polk* (Gloucester, MA: Peter Smith, 1967), 133.

44. Remini, *Webster*, 583; Crapol, *John Tyler*, 194; Frederick Merk, *History of the Westward Movement* (New York: Alfred A. Knopf, 1978), 281.

45. Isaac Van Zandt to Anson Jones, April 19, 1843, in *DCRT*, 2:164

46. Peterson, *Presidencies of William Henry Harrison and John Tyler*, 178–180.

47. Abel Upshur to John C. Calhoun, August 14, 1843, in *PJCC*, 17:356–357.

48. This exchange was originally printed in the *London Morning Chronicle* on August 19, 1843, but was included in full in a letter from Upshur to Everett. See Abel Upshur to Edward Everett, September 28, 1843, in *Diplomatic Correspondence of the United States: Inter-American Affairs, 1831–1860*, ed. William R. Manning (Washington, D.C.: Carnegie Endowment for International Peace, 1936), 7:8.

49. Abel Upshur to Edward Everett, September 28, 1843, in *DCUS*, 7:11.

50. Tyler, *Letters*, 2:389.

51. Merk, *Slavery*, 23–24.

52. Freehling, *Road to Disunion*, 371.

53. Merk, *Slavery*, 24.

54. Houston quoted in Gambrell, *Anson Jones*, 294; Pletcher, *Diplomacy of Annexation*, 128.

55. Anson Jones to Isaac Van Zandt, December 13, 1843, in *DCRT*, 2:233; Merk, *Slavery*, 25–26.

56. Sam Houston, "A Speech at the Old Capitol," November 10, 1843, in *WSH*, 3:456.

57. Peterson, *Presidencies of William Henry Harrison and John Tyler*, 192.

58. Pletcher, *Diplomacy of Annexation* 131; Hall, *Abel Parker Upshur*, 205–206; Peterson, *Presidencies of William Henry Harrison and John Tyler*, 199.

59. Pletcher, *Diplomacy of Annexation*, 132; Peterson, *Presidencies of William Henry Harrison and John Tyler*, 212.

60. Merk, *Slavery*, 48–49; Joel H. Silbey, *Storm Over Texas: The Annexation Controversy and the Road to Civil War* (Oxford: Oxford University Press, 2005), 33–35; Leahy, *President Without a Party*, 400–401.

61. Andrew Jackson to William B. Lewis, March 11, 1844, in *The Correspondence of Andrew Jackson*, ed. John Spencer Bassett (Washington, D.C.: Carnegie Institution of Washington, 1929), 6:272

62. Haley, *Sam Houston*, 279–280.

63. Sam Houston to Andrew Jackson, February 16, 1844, in *CAJ*, 6:261.

64. Sam Houston, "To the Texas Congress," January 20, 1844, in *WSH*, 3:523; Siegel, *Texas Republic*, 229–230.

65. Pletcher, *Diplomacy of Annexation*, 133.

66. Peterson, *Presidencies of William Henry Harrison and John Tyler*, 195.

67. Hall, *Abel Parker Upshur*, 211–213.

68. Van Zandt to Jones, March 5, 1844, in *DCRT*, 2:261–262.

69. Peterson, *Presidencies of William Henry Harrison and John Tyler*, 203.

70. For an example of Calhoun's arguments on states' rights and nullification see John C. Calhoun, "The Fort Hill Address: On the Relations of the States and Federal Government," in *Union and Liberty*, 367–400. For an example of Calhoun arguing that slavery constituted a positive good see John C. Calhoun, "Speech on the Introduction of His Resolutions on the Slave Question," in *Union and Liberty*, 511–522.

71. Monroe, *Republican Vision of John Tyler*, 38–45, 54–65; May, *John Tyler*, 105.

72. Peterson, *Presidencies of William Henry Harrison and John Tyler*, 205. See also May, *John Tyler*, 110.

73. John Tyler to Alexander Gardiner, June 17, 1847, in Tyler, *Letters*, 2:426.

74. Tyler to Gardiner, June 17, 1847, in Tyler, *Letters*, 2:426.

75. Peterson, *Presidencies of William Henry Harrison and John Tyler*, 204–206.

76. Monroe, *Republican Vision of John Tyler*, 173. For more on Calhoun's presidential ambitions see Joseph G. Rayback, "The Presidential Ambitions of John C. Calhoun, 1844–1848," *Journal of Southern History* 14, no. 3 (Aug. 1848): 331–356.

77. William M. Meigs, *The Life of John Caldwell Calhoun* (New York: Da Capo, 1970), 292; Peterson, *Presidencies of William Henry Harrison and John Tyler*, 211; Leahy, *President Without a Party*, 326–327.

78. John Tyler to John C. Calhoun, March 6, 1844, in *PJCC*, 17:828.

79. Meigs, *Life of John Caldwell Calhoun*, 292; May, *John Tyler*, 110; Pletcher, *Diplomacy of Annexation*, 135, n. 75.

80. For an example of Houston's concern see his letter to Anson Jones, April 6, 1844 in *WSH*, 4:295.

81. Leahy, *President Without a Party*, 328.

82. "The Treaty of Annexation," April 12, 1844, in *Documents of Texas History*, ed. Ernest Wallace, David M. Vigness, and George B. Ward (Austin, TX: State House Press, 1994), 143–144.

83. Sam Houston to Anson Jones, April 29, 1844, in *WSH*, 4:308.

84. Sam Houston to Van Zandt and Henderson, April 29, 1844, in *DCRT*, 2:275.

85. John Tyler to Andrew Jackson, April 18, 1844, in *CAJ*, 6:279. Another cause was to make sure a pro-annexation senator from Alabama was able to take his seat in time for the deliberations. Tyler had appointed Senator William King of Alabama as minister to France and Tyler wanted to ensure his replacement was in the Senate prior to the treaty debate. Additionally, Tyler refers to the letter from Pakenham as from Aberdeen, likely because Pakenham was forwarding Aberdeen's clarification of British policy.

86. John C. Calhoun to Richard Pakenham, April 27, 1844, in *DCUS*, 7:18–22.

87. John Tyler to Robert Tyler, April 17, 1850, in Tyler, *Letters*, 2:483.

88. John Tyler, "Message to the Senate of the United States," April 22, 1844, in James Daniel Richardson, comp., *The Compilation of the Messages and Papers of the Presidents* (New York: Bureau of National Literature 1909), 5:2160–2161.

89. John Tyler to Robert Tyler, April 17, 1850, in Tyler, *Letters*, 2:483.

90. Leahy, *President Without a Party*, 331.

91. Andrew Jackson to Francis P. Blair, May 11, 1844, in *CAJ*, 6:287.

92. John Quincy Adams, *Memoirs of John Quincy Adams: Comprising Portions of his Diary from 1795 to 1848*, ed. Charles Francis Adams (Philadelphia: J. B. Lippincott, 1876), 12:13–14. For further discussion of Northern Whig opposition and Northern Democrat hesitation see Freehling, *Road to Disunion*, 410.

93. See the letters from the Mexican Minister to the United States Juan Nepomuceno Almonte to Upshur, November 3, 1843, and November 11, 1843, in *Senate Documents*, 28th Congress, 1st session (341), 94–95, 97–99. For a more in-depth discussion of how Americans and Mexicans each viewed the Texas issue, see the correspondence between Waddy Thompson, American Minister to Mexico, and Jose Maria Bocanegra, Mexican Minister of Foreign Relations in *Senate Documents*, 28th Congress, 1st session (341), 89–93.

94. Tyler, "Third Annual Message," in Richardson, 5:2113.

95. Cash, "The Isolated Presidency," 47; Crapol, *John Tyler*, 217.

96. Gambrell, *Anson Jones*, 342; Theodore Roosevelt, *Thomas Hart Benton: American Statesman* (Boston: Houghton Mifflin, 1914), 263–267.

97. Merk, *Slavery*, 79. For Benton's three-day speech opposing annexation on May 16th, 18th, and 20th, see *Appendix to the Congressional Globe*, Senate, 28th Congress, 1st Session, 474–486. For his speech on June 1st see *Appendix to the Congressional Globe*, Senate, 28th Congress, 1st Session, 497–499.

98. Cash, "The Isolated Presidency," 48; Merk, *Slavery*, 81.

CHAPTER 5. THE ELECTIONS OF 1844

1. Michael F. Holt, *The Rise and Fall of the American Whig Party: Jacksonian Politics and the Onset of the Civil War* (Oxford: Oxford University Press, 1999), 172.

2. John Quincy Adams, *Memoirs of John Quincy Adams: Comprising Portions of his Diary from 1795 to 1848*, ed. Charles Francis Adams (Philadelphia: J.B. Lippincott, 1876), 12:22.

3. Henry Clay to the Editors of the Washington *Daily National Intelligencer* [Joseph Gales and William W. Seaton], April 17, 1844, in *The Papers of Henry Clay*, ed. Robert Seager II and Melba Porter Hay (Lexington, KY: University Press of Kentucky, 1988), 10:41–46.

4. Martin Van Buren to William Henry Hammett, April 20, 1844, http://vanburenpapers.org/document-mvb03868.

5. Andrew Jackson to the Editors of the Nashville *Union*, May 13, 1844, in *The Correspondence of Andrew Jackson*, ed. John Spencer Bassett (Washington, D.C.: Carnegie Institution of Washington, 1929), 6:289–291.

6. Andrew Jackson to Francis P. Blair, May 11, 1844, in *CAJ*, 6:286–287.

7. Holt, *Whig Party*, 172; "Whig Party Platform of 1844," May 1, 1844, https://www.presidency.ucsb.edu/documents/whig-party-platform-1844.

8. Ted Widmer, *Martin Van Buren* (New York: Times Books, 2005), 150–151.

9. William W. Freehling, *The Road to Disunion: Secessionists at Bay, 1776–1854* (Oxford: Oxford University Press, 1990), 429.

10. *Niles National Register (1837–1849)* 16, no. 14, Jun. 1, 1844, 211; Daniel Walker Howe, *What Hath God Wrought: The Transformation of America, 1815–1848* (Oxford: Oxford University Press, 2007), 683.

11. *Niles National Register (1837–1849)* 16, no. 14, Jun. 1, 1844, 211; Robert W. Merry, *A Country of Vast Designs: James K. Polk, the Mexican War, and the Conquest of the American Continent* (New York: Simon and Schuster, 2009), 90–95.

12. "1844 Democratic Party Platform," May 27, 1844, https://www.presidency.ucsb.edu/documents/1844-democratic-party-platform.

13. Merry, *County of Vast Designs*, 96.

14. Henry Clay to Stephen Miller, July 1, 1844, in *PHC*, 10:79.

15. Henry Clay to Thomas M. Peters and John M. Jackson, July 27, 1844, in *PHC*, 10:91.

16. Holt, *Whig Party*, 180.

17. Norma Lois Peterson, *The Presidencies of William Henry Harrison and John Tyler* (Lawrence, KS: University Press of Kansas, 1989), 225; Jordan T. Cash, "The Isolated Presidency: John Tyler and Unilateral Presidential Power," *American Political Thought* 7, no. 4 (Winter 2018): 39; Christopher J. Leahy, *President Without a Party: The Life of John Tyler* (Baton Rouge, LA: Louisiana State University Press, 2020), 332–333.

18. John Tyler to Henry Wise, in Lyon Gardiner Tyler, *The Letters and Times of the Tylers* (New York: Da Capo, 1970), 2:317.

19. Cash, "The Isolated Presidency," 48.

20. David M. Pletcher, *The Diplomacy of Annexation: Texas, Oregon, and the Mexican War* (Columbia, MO: University of Missouri Press, 1973), 149.

21. Andrew Jackson to James K. Polk, July 26, 1844, in *CAJ*, 6:304.

22. Merry, *Country of Vast Designs*, 102–103; Holt, *Whig Party*, 174–175; Peterson, *Presidencies of William Henry Harrison and John Tyler*, 238–239.

23. *Niles National Register, From March, 1844, to September, 1844* 66, ed. Jeremiah Hughes (Baltimore, MD: Exchange Place, 1844), 416.

24. *Niles National Register*, 417–418.

25. David A. Crockett, *The Oppositional Presidency: Leadership and the Constraints of History* (College Station, TX: Texas A&M University Press, 2002), 66; Peterson, *Presidencies of William Henry Harrison and John Tyler*, 238–239; Merry, *Country of Vast Designs*, 97–103.

26. Peterson, *Presidencies of William Henry Harrison and John Tyler*, 250.

27. Andrew Jackson to Major William B. Lewis, April 8, 1844, in *CAJ*, 6:278.

28. For an example of Houston's support see his letter to Jones on June 11, 1844, where he assures Jones that he has tremendous support. See Sam Houston to Anson Jones, June 11, 1844, in *The Writings of Sam Houston, 1813–1863*, ed. Amelia

W. Williams and Eugene C. Barker (Austin, TX: University of Texas Press, 1939), 4:331.

29. Stanley Siegel, *A Political History of the Texas Republic, 1836–1845* (Austin, TX: University of Texas Press, 1956), 236–237; Herbert Gambrell, *Anson Jones: The Last President of Texas*. (Austin, TX: University of Texas Press, 1964), 348.

30. Pletcher, *Diplomacy of Annexation*, 150–163.

31. Gambrell, *Anson Jones*, 350–352, 366.

32. Anson Jones, *Memoranda and Official Correspondence relating to the Republic of Texas, its History and Annexation* (New York: D. Appleton and Company, 1859), 54–55.

33. Jones quoted in Gambrell, *Anson Jones*, 359–360.

34. Siegel, *Texas Republic*, 234–235; Pletcher, *Diplomacy of Annexation*, 164–165.

35. Howe, *What Hath God*, 688–689; Merry, *Country of Vast Designs*, 110–111; Holt, *Whig Party*, 174–175.

36. Robert Seager II, *And Tyler Too: A Biography of John & Julia Gardiner Tyler* (New York: McGraw Hill, 1963), 241.

37. John Tyler, "Fourth Annual Message," December 3, 1844, https://miller center.org/the-presidency/presidential-speeches/december-3-1844-fourth-annu al-message.

38. Sarah Elizabeth Lewis, "Digest of Congressional Action on the Annexation of Texas December, 1844, to March, 1845," *Southwestern Historical Quarterly* 50, no. 2 (Oct. 1946): 253.

39. Albert Gallatin to D. Dudley Field, December 17, 1844, in *The Writings of Albert Gallatin*, ed. Henry Adams (New York: Antiquarian Press, 1960), 2:605–606. See also Gallatin's second letter to Field on February 10, 1845, which reiterates and expands on his arguments.

40. *Congressional Globe*, Senate, 28th Congress, 2nd Session, 304.

41. Adams, *Memoirs*, 12:174.

42. *Congressional Globe*, Senate, 28th Congress, 2nd Session, Appendix, 382.

43. *Congressional Globe*, House of Representatives, 28th Congress, 2nd Session, Appendix, 132.

44. Dan Monroe, *The Republican Vision of John Tyler* (College Station, TX: Texas A&M University Press, 2003), 163; Michael A. Morrison, *Slavery and the American West* (Chapel Hill, NC: University of North Carolina Press, 1997), 13–38.

45. Holt, *Whig Party*, 218–219.

46. Stephens quoted in Daniel Walker Howe, *The Political Culture of the American Whigs* (Chicago: University of Chicago Press, 1979), 242.

47. Robert Toombs to Alexander Stephens, January 24, 1845, in *Correspondence of Robert Toombs, Alexander H. Stephens, and Howell Cobb*, ed. Ulrich B. Phillips, (Washington, D.C.: Government Printing Office, 1913), 2:61.

48. Holt, *Whig Party*, 220; Lewis, "Digest of Congressional Action," 255.

49. Holt, *Whig Party*, 220–221; Peterson, *Presidencies of William Henry Harrison and John Tyler*, 255; Howe, *What Hath God*, 699.

50. Frederick Merk, *Slavery and the Annexation of Texas* (New York: Alfred A.

Knopf, 1972), 154; Peterson, *Presidencies of William Henry Harrison and John Tyler*, 256.

51. Peterson, *Presidencies of William Henry Harrison and John Tyler*, 256–257; Joel H. Silbey, *Storm Over Texas: The Annexation Controversy and the Road to Civil War* (Oxford: Oxford University Press, 2005), 86–88; Elbert B. Smith, *Magnificent Missourian: The Life of Thomas Hart Benton* (Westport, CT: Greenwood, 1957), 203; Howe, *What Hath God*, 698–699; Frederick Merk, *History of the Westward Movement* (New York: Alfred A. Knopf, 1978), 300–301; Merk, *Slavery*, 154–155.

52. For the full resolution see "The Resolution Annexing Texas to the United States," March 1, 1845, in *Documents of Texas History*, ed. Ernest Wallace, David M. Vigness, and George B. Ward (Austin, TX: State House Press, 1994), 146–147.

53. Holt, *Whig Party*, 221; Cash, "Isolated Presidency," 49.

54. Cash, "Isolated Presidency," 49.

55. See William R. King to John C. Calhoun, November 15, 1844, December 31, 1844, January 29, 1845, and February 27, 1845, in *Diplomatic Correspondence of the United States: Inter-American Affairs, 1831–1860*, ed. William R. Manning (Washington, D.C.: Carnegie Endowment for International Peace, 1936), 6:442–448.

56. Peterson, *Presidencies of William Henry Harrison and John Tyler*, 258.

57. Sam Houston, "Valedictory to the Texas Congress," December 9, 1844, in *WSH* 4:403. For his initial recommendation after the treaty's failure see Sam Houston, "Statement Concerning Annexation," July 1, 1844, in *WSH*, 4:336.

58. Sam Houston to Andrew Jackson, December 13, 1844, in *WSH*, 4:407.

59. Sam Houston, "Memorandum Setting Forth Terms for the Annexation of Texas to the United States," December 13, 1844, in *WSH*, 4:407–408.

60. Jones, *Memorandum*, 430.

61. Siegel, *Texas Republic*, 248–249.

62. Ashbel Smith, *Reminiscences of the Texas Republic* (Galveston, TX: Historical Society of Galveston, 1876), 81.

63. Sam Houston to Andrew Jackson Donelson, April 9, 1845, in *WSH*, 4:411.

64. Siegel, *Texas Republic*, 252.

65. "A Preliminary Treaty with Mexico," May 19, 1845, in *DTH*, 147.

66. Haley, *Sam Houston*, 291.

67. Smith, *Reminiscences*, 81.

68. "The Annexation Offer Accepted," July 4, 1845, in *DTH*, 148.

69. Haley, *Sam Houston*, 294–295.

70. Merry, *Country of Vast Designs*, 186–188; Sarah Burns, *The Politics of War Powers: The Theory and History of Presidential Unilateralism* (Lawrence, KS: University Press of Kansas, 2019), 108–110.

71. James K. Polk, "War Message to Congress," May 11, 1846, https://millercenter.org/the-presidency/presidential-speeches/may-11-1846-war-message-congress.

72. *Congressional Globe*, Senate, 29th Congress, 1st Session, 798.

73. Haley, *Sam Houston*, 292–360; Gregg Cantrell, "Sam Houston and the Know-Nothings: A Reappraisal," *Southwestern Historical Quarterly* 96, no. 3 (1993): 327–343.

74. Tyler, *Letters*, 2:546; Chris DeRose, *The Presidents' War: Six American Presidents and the Civil War That Divided Them* (Guilford, CT: Lyons Press, 2014), 105; Leahy, *President Without a Party*, 396; Edward P. Crapol, *John Tyler: The Accidental President* (Chapel Hill, NC: University of North Carolina Press, 2006), 255-256.

75. Crapol, *John Tyler*, 225-230.

76. Tyler, "Letter to the Editors of the *Richmond Enquirer*," May, 1847, in Tyler, *Letters*, 2:425; Crapol, *John Tyler*, 225-228.

77. Sam Houston, "Letter to F. L. Hatch," July 18, 1847, in *WSH*, 5:15-18.

78. John Tyler, "Letter to the Editors of the *Enquirer*," September 1, 1847, in Tyler, *Letters*, 2:428-431.

79. Sam Houston, "Letter to F. L. Hatch," October 20, 1847, in *WSH*, 5:20-27.

80. Crapol, *John Tyler*, 229-230; Tyler, *Letters*, 432-433.

81. Sam Houston, "Address at the Union Mass Meeting," September 22, 1860, in *WSH*, 8:151.

82. Sam Houston, "Message to the Texas Legislature," March 18, 1861, in *WSH*, 8:279

83. Haley, *Sam Houston*, 383-397.

84. John Tyler to Robert Tyler, August 27, 1860, in Tyler, *Letters*, 2:561.

85. Seager, *And Tyler Too*, 448-449; Crapol, *John Tyler*, 259-260; 403-404; DeRose, *Presidents' War*, 132-135.

86. "Amendments Proposed by the Peace Conference," February 8-27, 1861, https://avalon.law.yale.edu/19th_century/peace.asp.

87. Seager, *And Tyler Too*, 457-460.

88. Leahy, *President Without a Party*, 406-407; DeRose, *Presidents' War*, 146-148; Crapol, *John Tyler*, 264.

89. Crapol, *John Tyler*, 264-265.

90. Crapol, *John Tyler*, 264-265; DeRose, *Presidents' War*, 198-199.

91. DeRose, *Presidents' War*, 213.

CONCLUSION: THE PRIMACY OF PRESIDENTIAL POLICYMAKING

1. Alexander Hamilton, "Federalist 70," in Alexander Hamilton, James Madison, and John Jay, *The Federalist*, ed. J.R. Pole (Indianapolis, IN: Hackett, 2005), 376.

2. John Locke, *Two Treatises of Government*, ed. Peter Laslett (Cambridge: Cambridge University Press, 1988), 375.

3. For a sampling of the large and expansive literature on the relationship between the presidency and prerogative power see George Thomas, "As Far as Republican Principles Will Admit: Presidential Prerogative and Constitutional Government," *Presidential Studies Quarterly* 30, no. 3 (Sept. 2000): 534-552; Jeremy D. Bailey, "Executive Prerogative and the "Good Officer in Thomas Jefferson's Letter to John B. Colvin," *Presidential Studies Quarterly* 34, no. 4 (Dec. 2004): 732-754; Clement Fatovic, *Outside the Law: Emergency and Executive Power* (Baltimore, MD: John Hopkins University Press, 2009); Benjamin A. Kleinerman, *The Discretionary President: The Promise and Peril of Executive Power* (Lawrence,

KS: University Press of Kansas, 2009); David K. Nichols, "Lincoln: An Imperial President?" in *The Imperial Presidency and the Constitution*, ed. Gary J. Schmitt, Joseph M., Bessette, and Andrew E. Busch (Lanham, MD: Rowman and Littlefield, 2017): 5–22; Kevin J. Burns, *William Howard Taft's Constitutional Progressivism* (Lawrence, KS: University Press of Kansas, 2021); Jordan T. Cash, "George Sutherland and the Contextualization of Executive Power," *American Political Thought* 9, no. 1 (Winter 2020): 76.

4. Houston to Jackson, August 11, 1838, in *The Writings of Sam Houston, 1813–1863*, ed. Amelia W. Williams and Eugene C. Barker (Austin, TX: University of Texas Press, 1939), 2:271.

5. Herbert Gambrell, *Anson Jones: The Last President of Texas* (Austin, TX: University of Texas Press, 1964), 353.

6. James Madison, "Federalist 10," in *The Federalist*, 53.

7. This turnover also resulted in three additional men also serving as interim secretaries of state in between the tenures of Webster, Upshur, and Calhoun. Specifically, Attorney General Hugh Legaré served after Webster's resignation, but died in June 1843 before Upshur was confirmed, at which point the State Department Clerk William S. Derrick served in the position for a few days until Upshur took up the post. When Upshur was later killed, Attorney General John Nelson became the interim secretary for about a month until Calhoun's appointment and confirmation. As none of these three was a permanent secretary of state and did not have a major impact on Texas policy, I have not included them in the main discussion of Tyler's diplomacy.

8. Alexander Hamilton, "Federalist 71," in *The Federalist*, 383.

9. Alexander Hamilton, "Federalist 72," in *The Federalist*, 387.

10. For a description of the first-mover advantage see William G. Howell, *Power without Persuasion: The Politics of Direct Presidential Action* (Princeton: Princeton University Press, 2003), 27. For its application to Tyler's foreign policy see Jordan T. Cash, "The Isolated Presidency: John Tyler and Unilateral Presidential Power," *American Political Thought* 7, no. 4 (Winter 2018): 43. For the quote see Alexander Hamilton, "Pacificus I," in Alexander Hamilton and James Madison, *The Pacificus-Helvidius Debates of 1793-1794: Toward the Completion of the American Founding*, ed. Morton J. Frisch (Indianapolis, IN: Liberty Fund, 2007), 15.

11. J. David Alvis, Jeremy D. Bailey, and F. Flagg Taylor IV, *The Contested Removal Power, 1789–2010* (Lawrence: University Press of Kansas, 2013), 67–99.

12. Interestingly, Tyler's use of secret service funds relating to the Webster-Ashburton Treaty with Great Britain was later the subject of a congressional investigation after Tyler left office, although he was ultimately exonerated. His use of those funds relating to Texas, however, were not investigated by Congress. See Christopher J. Leahy, *President Without a Party: The Life of John Tyler* (Baton Rouge, LA: Louisiana State University Press, 2020), 280; Cash, "Isolated Presidency," 45.

13. Sam Houston, "Letter to F. L. Hatch," October 20, 1847, in *WSH*, 5:26.

14. William S. McFeely, *Grant: A Biography* (New York: W. W. Norton, 1982),

350. See also Millery Polyné, "Expansion Now!: Haiti, "Santo Domingo," and Frederick Douglass at the Intersection of U.S. and Caribbean Pan-Americanism," *Caribbean Studies* 34, no. 2 (July-December, 2006): 3-45.

15. Edward P. Crapol, *John Tyler: The Accidental President* (Chapel Hill, NC: University of North Carolina Press, 2006), 280; William Javier Nelson, *Almost a Territory: America's Attempt to Annex the Dominican Republic* (Wilmington, DE: University of Delaware Press, 1990), 85; Charles C. Tansill, "War Powers of the President of the United States with Special Reference to the Beginning of Hostilities," *Political Science Quarterly* 45, no. 1 (Mar. 1930): 41-47.

16. Cash, "Isolated Presidency," 46; Crapol, *John Tyler*, 130.

17. Homer E. Socolofsky and Allan B. Spetter, *The Presidency of Benjamin Harrison* (Lawrence, KS: University Press of Kansas, 1987), 200-205; Richard E. Welch, *The Presidencies of Grover Cleveland* (Lawrence, KS: University Press of Kansas, 1988), 169-175; Tennant S. McWilliams, "James H. Blount, the South, and Hawaiian Annexation," *Pacific Historical Review* 57, no. 1 (1988): 25-46.

18. McKinley quoted in Howard Wayne Morgan, *William McKinley and his America* (Kent, OH: Kent State University Press, 2003), 225.

19. Crapol, *John Tyler*, 280; Lewis Gould, *The Presidency of William McKinley* (Lawrence, KS: University Press of Kansas, 1980), 49-50, 56, 98-99.

20. Cash, "Isolated Presidency," 28; Stephen Skowronek, *Building a New American State: The Expansion of National Administrative Capacities, 1877-1920* (Cambridge: Cambridge University Press, 1982).

21. George B. Erath, *The Memoirs of Major George B. Erath, 1813-1891*, ed. Lucy Erath (Waco, TX: Heritage Society of Waco, 1956), 78.

22. Jeffrey K. Tulis, *The Rhetorical Presidency* (Princeton: Princeton University Press, 1987), 25-87.

23. Cash, "Isolated Presidency," 48.

24. Samuel Kernell, *Going Public: New Strategies of Presidential Leadership* (Washington, D.C.: CQ Press, 2007).

25. Stanley Siegel, *A Political History of the Texas Republic, 1836-1845* (Austin, TX: University of Texas Press, 1956), 253.

BIBLIOGRAPHIC ESSAY

Examining the annexation of Texas from the perspective of the American and Texian presidencies necessarily involves addressing several different areas of scholarly literature.

With regard to annexation itself, there are a plethora of works examining Texas' addition to the Union. Most of these examine the controversy over Texas primarily from the American perspective, often in the broader context of antebellum politics and situating Texas' admission to the United States as contributing to the conditions that ultimately led to the Civil War. Joel H. Silbey's *Storm Over Texas: The Annexation Controversy and the Road to Civil War* (Oxford: Oxford University Press, 2005) is the most recent and representative of this scholarship, covering annexation in the first half and using the back half of the work to discuss the fallout from Texas joining the Union. Other histories and studies of antebellum America have included Texas' annexation as a major pivot point in nineteenth-century American politics. William W. Freehling's *The Road to Disunion: Secessionists at Bay, 1776-1854* (Oxford: Oxford University Press, 1990) and Daniel Walker Howe's *What Hath God Wrought: The Transformation of America, 1815-1848* (Oxford: Oxford University Press, 2007) are the two most prominent surveys of antebellum America that pay substantial attention to annexation as a major event. Notably, Howe includes the Texas Revolution and aspects of Texas' history as an independent nation as part of his broader survey of American history, and by ending in 1848 with the end of the Mexican War, he implicitly highlights Texas' annexation and the resulting war as the events which shifted the United States from the politics of the Jacksonian era to the increasingly contentious debate over slavery.

Similarly, scholarly evaluations of the United States' westward expansion have necessarily included discussions of Texas. Frederick Merk's *History of the Westward Movement* (New York: Alfred A. Knopf, 1978) is the most prominent example, and adds to his earlier work *Slavery and the Annexation of Texas* (New York: Alfred A. Knopf, 1972), which, as the name suggests, focused exclusively on annexation and the central role played by slavery in the arguments of both proponents and opponents of annexation. In the latter volume on annexation and slavery, Merk also includes a variety of invaluable original sources, including presidential and congressional speeches as well as letters from some of the major figures. Several other works on westward expansion do not deal directly with annexation but show how earlier efforts such as the Louisiana Purchase and Missouri Compromise laid the groundwork for the United States to expand to the West and created the conditions for slavery to be a major cleavage point in the debate over Texas. Specifically, Jon Kukla's *A Wilderness So Immense: The Louisiana Purchase and the Destiny of America* (New York: Alfred A. Knopf, 2003) and William S. Belko's *Contesting the Constitution: Congress Debates the Missouri Crisis, 1819-1820* (Columbia, MO: University of Missouri Press, 2021) cover the major arguments and issues at the core of the Louisiana Purchase and Missouri Compromise, many of which would later be reflected in the debates over Texas annexation.

Annexation also factors as a major event in American diplomatic history. In understanding the motivations and decisions undergirding annexation, the original correspondence collected and edited by William R. Manning as *Diplomatic Correspondence of the United States* (Washington: Carnegie Endowment for International Peace, 1936) is invaluable. The collections of the papers of Secretaries of State Daniel Webster—both *The Diplomatic and Official Papers of Daniel Webster While Secretary of State* (New York: Harper and Brothers Publishers, 1848), and *The Papers of Daniel Webster* (ed. Harold D. Moser. Hanover, NH: University Press of New England, 1982)—and John C. Calhoun—*The Papers of John C. Calhoun* (ed. Ross M. Lence. Indianapolis, IN: Liberty Fund, 1992)—similarly provide significant insight into what drove American diplomacy during this period as Webster and Calhoun corresponded with American diplomats as well as their counterparts in Europe and Mexico. Moreover, given Webster's opposition to annexation and Calhoun's support of it, these collections further allow us to see the competing visions of American foreign policy that divided the Tyler administration and grant us a view into how officials in Texas, Europe, and Mexico addressed the question of annexation. Even the *Correspondence of Andrew Jackson* (Washington, D.C.: Carnegie Institution of Washington, 1929), edited by John Spencer Bassett, contains a wealth of information and insight, despite Jackson being a retired private citizen when annexation took place.

On the European side, Ephraim Douglass Adams' *British Diplomatic Correspondence Concerning the Republic of Texas, 1838-1846* (Austin, TX: The Texas State Historical Association, 1917) provides a window into the British perspective on Texas and how the Lone Star Republic fit into Britain's larger grand strategy in the Americas. Similarly, George Garrison's *Diplomatic Correspondence of the Republic of Texas* (Washington: Government Printing Office, 1908) and the collection of *Memoranda and Official Correspondence relating to the Republic of Texas, its History and Annexation* (New York: D. Appleton and Company, 1859) by the last president of Texas, Anson Jones, provide first-hand accounts of the Texians' strategy for annexation, including attempts to leverage European interests against both the Americans and the Mexicans.

In terms of the secondary literature on American diplomacy, the most complete account of annexation and the push westward to make the United States a fully continental nation is David M. Pletcher's *The Diplomacy of Annexation: Texas, Oregon, and the Mexican War* (Columbia, MO: University of Missouri Press, 1973). As the title suggests, Pletcher examines not only the diplomatic machinations that brought Texas into the Union, but also the wrangling over setting the boundary of the Oregon territory, demonstrating not only the specifics in each case, but how they are connected as part of a general American diplomatic agenda. Jesse S. Reeves's work on *American Diplomacy under Tyler and Polk* (Gloucester, MA: Peter Smith, 1967), is similarly wide-ranging, covering the major diplomatic issues of the 1840s and the expansion of the United States. Matthew Karp's *This Vast Southern Empire: Slaveholders at the Helm of American Foreign Policy* (Cambridge, MA: Harvard University Press, 2016) does not directly focus on Texas, but shows how annexation was a major policy initiative for supporters of slavery.

From the Texian perspective, Joseph William Schmitz's work *Texan Statecraft, 1836-1845* (San Antonio: The Naylor Company, 1941) does an excellent job laying out the foreign policy and grand strategy of the Republic of Texas from its founding to annexation. Other works which place Texas more at the center of American antebellum foreign policy include Richard Bruce Winder's *Crisis in the Southwest: The United*

States, Mexico, and the Struggle over Texas (Wilmington, DE: SR Books, 2002), which takes account of the intense diplomatic maneuverings of the Americans, Texians, and Mexicans.

When it comes to the Republic of Texas itself, the definitive account of the Lone Star Republic's political history remains Stanley Siegel's *A Political History of the Texas Republic, 1836–1845* (Austin, TX: University of Texas Press, 1956). Siegel provides a detailed description of the major players and issues affecting Texas politics from independence to annexation, fully bringing out the vibrancy of Texian politics. Siegel also ably touches on the broader international issues which influenced Texian politics, particularly its relations with the United States, Mexico, Britain, and France. For a broader survey of Texas beyond its explicitly historical aspects and outside the republican period, Clarence R. Wharton's *History of Texas* (Dallas: Turner Company, 1935), is a good introduction. For discussions of the Texas Revolution, Stephen L. Harden's *Texian Iliad: A Military History of the Texas Revolution* (Austin, TX: University of Texas Press, 1996) is the most comprehensive modern account of the military aspects of the revolution, while Paul D. Lack's *The Texas Revolutionary Experience: A Political and Social History, 1835–1836* (College Station, TX: Texas A&M University Press, 1992) provides a detailed assessment of the political dimension. In particular, Lack gives us substantive descriptions of the ad hoc government the Texians assembled as well as the work to declare independence and create a new national constitution. A more recent account is William C. Davis's *Lone Star Rising: The Revolutionary Birth of the Texas Republic* (College Station, TX: Texas A&M University Press, 2006), which covers similar ground. For a particularly meticulous account of the formation of the Texas constitution, see also Rupert N. Richardson, "Framing the Constitution of the Republic of Texas," *The Southwestern Historical Quarterly* 31, no. 3 (Jan. 1928), 191–220. Beyond the revolutionary and republican periods, Randolph Campbell in *An Empire for Slavery: The Peculiar Institution in Texas, 1821–1865* (Baton Rouge, LA: Louisiana State University Press, 1989) and Andrew J. Torget's *Seeds of Empire: Cotton, Slavery, and the Transformation of the Texas Borderlands, 1800–1850* (Chapel Hill, NC: University of North Carolina Press, 2015) both highlight the importance of slavery in Texas to not only the independence movement, but also to the politicians governing the independent Republic of Texas as well as to the proponents of annexation.

Additionally, there are several collections of original sources covering the Texas Revolution and subsequent Republic of Texas, including not only public papers such as the Texas Declaration of Independence, the Texas Constitution, and the Treaty of Velasco which ended the revolution, but also private letters of the major players. Of these collections, the most significant are *Documents of Texas History* (Austin, TX: State House Press, 1994) edited by Ernest Wallace, David M. Vigness, and George B. Ward; *The Laws of Texas, 1822–1897* (Austin, TX: Gammel Book Company, 1898), compiled by H. P. H. Gammel; and *The Papers of the Texas Revolution, 1835–1836* (Austin, TX: Presidial Press, 1973), edited by John Holmes Jenkins, James H. Sutton Jr., and Sylvia Leal Carvajal. Sam Houston's papers, which have been collected and edited by Amelia W. Williams and Eugene C. Barker into eight volumes titled *The Writings of Sam Houston, 1813–1863* (Austin, TX: The University of Texas Press, 1939) are also an indispensable resource for seeing how the Texas government operated at the highest levels.

Yet to understand Texas and the conditions in which it declared independence and then operated as an independent nation, it is important not only to consider Texas itself and the United States, but also the early history of the Mexican republic. The entire period of Mexico's history just before independence to after the war with the United States is covered in Jaime E. Rodriguez Ordóñez's edited volume *The Origins of Mexican National Politics, 1808–1847* (Wilmington, DE: Scholarly Resources, Inc., 1997). Stanley C. Green's book *The Mexican Republic: The First Decade, 1823–1832* (Pittsburgh, PA: University of Pittsburgh Press, 1995) covers Mexican history from the fall of the First Mexican Empire which formed after independence to the rise of Santa Anna. Michael P. Costeloe then picks up the narrative in his work *The Central Republic in Mexico, 1835–1846: 'Hombres de Bien' in the Age of Santa Anna* (Cambridge: Cambridge University Press, 2002). Costeloe's book addresses the Texas Revolution but situates the Texians' efforts within the larger context of Mexican politics, highlighting the simultaneous revolutions in other parts of Mexico that constituted the broader "Federalist War" against the centralized government of Santa Anna. Timothy J. Henderson's *A*

Glorious Defeat: Mexico and Its War with the United States (New York: Hill and Wang, 2007) covers primarily the aftermath of annexation. An interesting original source which grants us a Mexican perspective of the United States is Lorenzo de Zavala's *Journey to the United States of North America* (Houston: Arte Público Press, 2005), translated by Wallace Woolsey. As I note in chapter one, Zavala was a major Mexican statesman intimately involved with the founding of the Republic of Texas. For readers who might wish to have a better understanding of the self-proclaimed "Napoleon of the West," Will Fowler's *Santa Anna of Mexico* (Lincoln, NE: University of Nebraska Press, 2007) is the most recent comprehensive biography of the Mexican general and dictator.

Of course, in the present work, Santa Anna is a secondary player, and the two presidents of greater interest are American president John Tyler and Texas president Sam Houston. Tyler has previously been a subject of presidential biographies but has received more scholarly interest in recent years. Tyler's own son, Lyon Gardiner Tyler, collected his father's correspondence and put them together with commentary to provide a detailed, although at times hagiographic, account of his father's political career, calling it *The Letters and Times of the Tylers* (New York: Da Capo Press, 1970). The first scholarly biography of Tyler was Robert J. Morgan's relatively short volume *A Whig Embattled: The Presidency Under John Tyler* (Lincoln, NE: University of Nebraska Press, 1954). Another early biography, Oliver Chitwood's *John Tyler: Champion of the Old South* (New York: Russell and Russell, Inc., 1964), emphasized the president's connections to the Virginia aristocracy. Yet perhaps the most comprehensive biography of Tyler remains Robert Seager II's book which carries the somewhat dismissive title *And Tyler Too: A Biography of John & Julia Gardiner Tyler* (New York: McGraw Hill Book Company, 1963). As the title suggests, however, this biography is not solely of Tyler, but also of his second wife, and as a result spends a considerable amount of time on Tyler's family life. In the recent scholarship on Tyler, Dan Monroe provides an excellent overview of Tyler's political thought in *The Republican Vision of John Tyler* (College Station, TX: Texas A&M University Press, 2003), while Edward P. Crapol's *John Tyler: The Accidental President* (Chapel Hill, NC: University of North Carolina Press, 2006) covers Tyler's life but takes particular interest in Tyler's foreign policy, including his actions regarding Texas. Among other biographies, Gary May's *John Tyler* (New York: Henry Hold and Company, 2008), is the shortest and most concise book-length overview of Tyler's life and career. The most recent biography is the much more detailed *President without a Party: The Life of John Tyler* (Baton Rouge, LA: Louisiana State University Press, 2020), written by Christopher J. Leahy. Leahy does a nice job of seamlessly weaving in between the personal and political parts of Tyler's life.

As the major figure of early Texas politics, Sam Houston has also received considerable attention from biographers. The earliest scholarly account of Houston's life is James Marquis' *The Raven: A Biography of Sam Houston* (New York: Blue Ribbon Books, 1929), while the most recent, and as of this writing the most definitive, biography of Houston is James Haley's work simply titled *Sam Houston* (Norman, OK: University of Oklahoma Press, 2002). Other than full biographies, particular aspects of Houston's life have been subject to scholarly inquiry, such as Jack Gregory and Rennard Stickland's *Sam Houston with the Cherokees, 1829–1833* (Norman, OK: University of Oklahoma Press, 1995), Gregg Cantrell's study of Houston's partisan affiliations in "Sam Houston and the Know Nothings: A Reappraisal," *Southwestern Historical Quarterly* 96, no. 3 (1993): 327–343; and Elizabeth Cook's investigation into Houston's failed marriage to Eliza Allen in "Sam Houston and Eliza Allen: The Marriage and the Mystery," *Southwestern Historical Quarterly* 94, no. 1 (Jul., 1990): 1–36.

Other than Tyler and Houston, the biographies of other major figures help to shed further light on the major issues affecting annexation. The most prominent are Claude H. Hall's biography of Tyler's second secretary of state, *Abel Parker Upshur: Conservative Virginian 1790–1844* (Madison, WI: State Historical Society of Wisconsin, 1964); David S. Heidler and Jeanne T. Heidler's co-authored account of Henry Clay's life, *Henry Clay: The Essential American* (New York: Random House, 2010)—as well as *The Papers of Henry Clay* (Lexington, KY: The University Press of Kentucky, 1988), edited by Robert Seager II and Melba Porter Hay—Robert Remini's biographies *Andrew Jackson: The Course of American Democracy, 1833–1845* (Baltimore, MD: Johns Hopkins University Press, 1998), *Daniel Webster: The Man and His Time* (New York: W. W.

Norton, 1997), and *Martin Van Buren and the Making of the Democratic Party* (New York: Columbia University Press, 1959); Theodore Roosevelt's *Thomas Hart Benton: American Statesman* (Boston: Houghton Mifflin Company, 1914); Paul A. Varg's *Edward Everett: The Intellectual in the Turmoil of Politics* (Selinsgrove, PA: Susquehanna University Press, 1992); and finally Robert W. Merry's *A Country of Vast Designs: James K. Polk, the Mexican War, and the Conquest of the American Continent* (New York: Simon and Schuster, 2009).

Yet even while those additional biographies are helpful in showing how other individuals played a role in the drama of annexation, the core of this book is about the two presidents, Tyler and Houston, and what they tell us about executive power. As a result, this book relies heavily on the expansive literature concerning the presidency. The University Press of Kansas' American Presidency Series has been particularly important to presidential studies, and this book drew from several volumes in that series, including Norma Lois Peterson's *The Presidencies of William Henry Harrison and John Tyler* (Lawrence, KS: University Press of Kansas, 1989); Major L. Wilson's *The Presidency of Martin Van Buren* (Lawrence, KS: University Press of Kansas, 1984); Mary W. M. Hargreaves' *The Presidency of John Quincy Adams* (Lawrence, KS: University Press of Kansas, 1985); Donald B. Cole's *The Presidency of Andrew Jackson* (Lawrence, KS: University Press of Kansas, 1993); Homer E. Socolofsky and Allan B. Spetter's *The Presidency of Benjamin Harrison* (Lawrence, KS: University Press of Kansas, 1987); and Lewis Gould's *The Presidency of William McKinley* (Lawrence, KS: University Press of Kansas, 1980).

While the aforementioned books are historical accounts of those presidencies, for works more explicitly focused on the extent of presidential power, William G. Howell's *Power without Persuasion: The Politics of Direct Presidential Action* (Princeton: Princeton University Press, 2003) is a seminal work on unilateral presidential power. There is also a growing literature on the presidency's expansive constitutional authority. Of particular note are Benjamin A. Kleinerman's *The Discretionary President: The Promise and Peril of Executive Power* (Lawrence, KS: University Press of Kansas, 2009), Jeffrey K. Tulis's *The Rhetorical Presidency* (Princeton: Princeton University Press, 1987), Michael J.

Gerhardt's *The Forgotten Presidents: Their Untold Constitutional Legacy* (Oxford: Oxford University Press, 2013), and my own work *The Isolated Presidency* (Oxford: Oxford University Press, 2023).

Drawing from these various scholarly sources, this book contributes and extends the many diverse strands of research concerning Texas history and annexation, American foreign policy, and presidential power.

INDEX

Aberdeen, Lord, 57, 59–60, 66
Adams, John Quincy
    Adams-Onís Treaty and, 31
    annexation viewpoint of, 44, 52
    candidacy of, 21
    John Tyler's support for, 22
    resolution viewpoint of, 81
    Texas acquisition attempts of, 33
Adams-Onís Treaty, 31, 33
admissions clause, 76, 80, 101
Alabama, constitution drafting in, 7
Alamo, fall of, 6, 38
Allen, Eliza, 36
American Party, 87–88
annexation, of Hawaii, 101–102
annexation, of Texas
    admissions clause and, 76, 80, 101
    aftermath of, 86–87
    American congressional resolution regarding, 80
    constitutional innovations and provisions regarding, 100–102
    constitutional variance regarding, 97–100
    debate regarding, 40, 52–53, 59, 61–62, 80–86, 96–97
    European option regarding, 54–58
    Mexican conflict regarding, 43
    opposition to, 105
    political contexts regarding, 102–105
    public support for, 104
    sectionalism and, 68, 71
    stalling of, 42–47, 60–61
    structural differences regarding, 93–97
    support for, 62
    tensions regarding, 51–52
    Texas congressional resolution regarding, 44
    treaty of, 65–66, 66–69, 98–99
    voting regarding, 83
Anti-Federalists, 9, 10, 16
Army of Texas, 6, 38
Austin, Stephen F., 33, 39

Battle of San Jacinto, 38–39
Benton, Thomas Hart, 68, 69, 82–83
Birney, James G., 79
Blair, Francis, 73
Britain
    abolition viewpoint of, 57–58
    accusations regarding, 51–52
    annexation viewpoint of, 54–55, 66–67, 77, 84
    Diplomatic Act of, 99
    John Tyler's concerns regarding, 96
    as mediator, 56, 85, 88–89
    Mexican support by, 124–125n38
    slavery viewpoint of, 124n36
    Texas recognition and, 55–57
    Webster-Ashburton Treaty and, 53
Brown, Milton, 82
Buchanan, James, 73
Burleson, Edward, 77
Butler, Anthony, 34

cabinet, of John Tyler, 28
Calhoun, John C., 23, 58, 63–67, 81
Campbell, Randolph, 2
Carson, Samuel P., 110–111n5
Cass, Lewis, 74
Childress, George C., 7
Choate, Rufus, 81
Civil War, 1–2, 91
Clay, Henry
    "Alabama letters" of, 75, 79
    annexation viewpoint of, 70, 71, 75, 105
    appointment of, 21
    candidacy of, 21
    influence of, 35
    John Tyler and, 26, 28, 29
    Louisiana Purchase viewpoint of, 71
    Missouri Compromise and, 19
    nomination of, 70–71, 73, 74–75
    resolutions of, 13, 14
    Texas acquisition attempts of, 33
    Whig Party and, 26, 73
Cleveland, Grover, 101

146 INDEX

Clopton, John, 17
Coahuila y Tejas, 8, 10, 13, 32
Compromise of 1850, 87
Congress (Texas)
    trust in Houston by, 94
    war declaration by, 50, 95
Congress (U. S.)
    annexation role of, 44
    "Era of Good Feelings" in, 17, 21
    "Jackson party" in, 22
    John Tyler and, 29, 30, 102–103
    lame duck session of, 79–86
    Old Republicans in, 17
    state admission role of, 18
Constitution, 6–15
Constitutional Convention (Texas), 6–7
Consultation, 37, 38
Cranch, William, 27
Crapol, Edward, 19
Crawford, William, 21
Crockett, David, 2
Cuervas, Luis, 85

Davis, Jefferson, 92
Declaration of Independence (Texas), 111n8
Democratic Party, 21, 43, 73–74, 81
Democratic-Republican Party, 21, 75
Derrick, William S., 132n7
diffusion, theory of, 19
Diplomatic Act (Britain), 78–79, 99
Dominican Republic, 100–101
Donelson, Andrew Jackson, 83, 85
Douglass, Frederick, 2

elections of 1844, 70–79
Electoral College, 12, 36
Elliot, Charles, 56–57, 124n36
Ellis, Richard, 110–111n5
empresarios, 32–33
Everett, Edward, 52, 105

Federalist 10, 96
Federalist 77, 12
Federalist Party, 17
Federalist War, 139
filibusters, 32

Florida, 22
Force Bill, 23
Forsyth, John, 43
France, 55–56, 77, 84
Freehling, William, 1–2, 56, 73

Gallatin, Albert, 80
Gilmer, Thomas Walker, 52
Goliad, capture of, 49
Grant, Ulysses S., 2, 100–101
Grayson, Peter, 43
Green, Duff, 59
Guizot, François, 54
Gutiérrez de Lara, Bernardo, 32
Gutiérrez-Magee Expedition, 32

Hamilton, Alexander, 12, 94
Harrison, Benjamin, 101
Harrison, William Henry, 25, 26–27, 28
Hawaii, annexation of, 101–102
Henderson, James Pinckney, 45, 65, 86
Henderson, John, 68
Hendrickson, Kenneth, 47
Henry, Patrick, 16
Holt, Michael, 75, 82
House of Representatives, 21, 35–36, 42, 44, 80–83. *See also* Congress (U. S.)
Houston, Sam
    Andrew Jackson and, 35–36
    after annexation, 87–90
    annexation viewpoint of, 3, 49, 60–61, 62–63, 103–104
    Army of Texas and, 6, 38
    assessing, 106–107
    background of, 34–35
    Battle of San Jacinto and, 38–39
    Cherokee tribe and, 34, 37
    Compromise of 1850 and, 87
    Congressional trust in, 94
    as Congressman, 35
    constitutional authority of, 45
    death of, 90
    defensive war strategy of, 49
    diplomacy of, 51, 53, 55, 59, 96
    Diplomatic Act (Britain) and, 78
    election of, 40, 47, 48, 97, 102
    European option and, 54–58

executive power of, 94
farewell address of, 84
as fighting for recognition, 40–42
as governor of Tennessee, 36–37
as governor of Texas, 88
immigration of, 37
inaugural address of, 40
influence of, 3–4
injuries of, 39
John Tyler and, 88–89
Kansas-Nebraska Act and, 87
leadership challenges of, 93–94, 106
leadership characteristics of, 95–96
marriage and divorce of, 36–37
military service of, 34–35
negotiations by, 57, 98
popularity of, 4, 102, 103
as "The Raven," 34–39
removal power provision and, 99
as Senator, 86
as strategist, 94
treaty viewpoint of, 65–66
veto of, 50, 95
war viewpoint of, 49–50
Houston, Samuel, Sr., 34
Hunt, Memucan, Jr., 43–44

immigration, to Texas, 32–33, 41
impeachment, standards for, 9

Jackson, Andrew
  annexation viewpoint of, 40–42, 62, 72–73, 105
  candidacy of, 21
  Democratic Party and, 72–73
  election of, 22
  Force Bill and, 23
  John Tyler and, 22–24, 25
  Martin Van Buren and, 72–73
  national bank and, 23–24
  removal power and, 12–13, 14
  Sam Houston and, 35–36
  Santa Anna and, 41
  support for, 21
  Texas acquisition attempts of, 33–34
  viewpoint of, 12
Jefferson, Thomas, 16, 19, 20, 31
Johnson, Richard Mentor, 74

Jones, Anson
  annexation viewpoint of, 51, 78, 85–86
  appointment of, 44–45
  candidacy of, 77
  Diplomatic Act (Britain) and, 78–79
  leadership of, 85
  removal conflict regarding, 99
  retirement of, 86
judges, appointment of, 11

Kansas-Nebraska Act, 87
King, William, 84, 126n85

Lack, Paul, 6–7
Lamar, Mirabeau, 45–47
Leahy, Christopher, 18, 67
Legaré, Hugh, 132n7
"Lexington of Texas," 37
Liberia, 111n6
Liberty Party, 79
Liliuokalani, Queen of Hawaii, 101
Lincoln, Abraham, 89, 91
Locke, John, 94
Long, James, 32
Long Filibuster, 32
Louisiana Purchase, 31, 71

Madison, Bishop James, 16
Madison, James, 12, 16, 19, 96
Madisonian (newspaper), 103
Magee, Augustus, 32
Maine, as free state, 19
Mangum, Willie Person, 25
manifest destiny, 1
Marshall, John, 16
McDuffie, George, 80
McKinley, William, 101–102
McMinn, Joseph, 35
Mexican Constitution
  drafting of, 7
  influence of, 14–15
  presidential election and, 11
  presidential military powers of, 10
  presidential reelection of, 9
  presidential removal power in, 13
  removal power in, 13
  repeal of, 37

Mexican War, 1, 86–87
Mexico
    annexation viewpoint of, 68, 77
    British financial support to, 124–125n38
    constitution of, 7
    dictatorship in, 15
    empresarios and, 32–33
    incursions from, 49, 50, 86–87, 94
    independence of, 32
    influences to, 7
    mediation refusal by, 56
    proposal by, 57
    threats from, 68
    treaty offer from, 85–86
    uprisings in, 38
    war declaration against, 50, 95
    war strategy regarding, 49
Mier, conflict in, 50–51
military, 10, 23
Missouri, 7, 17–18, 19
Missouri Compromise, 18–19
Monroe, Dan, 18, 64
Monroe, James, 16, 19
Monroe Doctrine, 96
Murphy, William Sumter, 62

national bank, 23–24, 29
National Intelligencer (newspaper), 71
Navarro, José Antonio, 7
Nelson, John, 132n7
New Mexico, Texas' claims regarding, 46
Niles National Register (newspaper), 76–77
North Carolina, constitution drafting in, 7
Nullification Crisis, 23

Old Republicans, in U. S. Congress, 17
Oolooteka (Cherokee leader), 34
Ordóñez, Jaime Rodríguez, 13
Oregon Territory, 53, 62, 87

Pakenham, Richard, 66–67
Palmer, Martin, 110–111n5
Peterson, Norma, 64
Poinsett, Joel R., 33
Polk, James K., 74, 77, 79–86, 103, 104, 106

Potter, Robert, 110n5
presidents
    appointment power of, 11
    constitutional description of, 8–15
    constitutional practice and, 4
    election standards of, 11–12
    impeachment standards for, 9
    limitations of, 15
    military powers of, 10, 100–101
    prerogative power of, 94
    reelection of, 9
    removal power of, 12, 13–14, 99
    requirements of, 8–9
    term length of, 9, 97
    turnover in, 97
    vacancy of, 27
    See also specific persons
Provincias Internas, Texas in, 32

Randolph, Edmund, 17
Randolph, John, 20, 35
Rathbun, George, 81
Refugio, capture of, 49
Reily, James, 51, 53, 54
representatives, term length of, 9
Rives, William C., 81
Ruiz, José Francisco, 7

San Antonio, capture of, 49, 50
Santa Anna, Antonio López de, 15, 38–39, 41, 42, 57
Santa Fe, 46–47
secession
    of Texas, 90
    of Virginia, 91
sectionalism, 68, 71
Senate, 9, 14, 66–69, 82–83. *See also* Congress (U. S.)
Siegel, Stanley, 48, 49
Silbey, Joel, 2
slavery, 2, 18–19, 40–41, 57–58, 59–60, 124n36
Smith, Ashbel, 51, 57–58, 85–86, 124n36
Smith, Henry, 39
Somervell, Alexander, 50
Spain, Texas and, 32
Spencer, John, 68
Spitzer, Robert, 3

INDEX 149

Stephens, Alexander, 81
Stevenson, Andrew, 17

Tallmadge, James, 17–18
Taylor, Zachary, 86
Tennessee, Houston as governor of, 36–37
Texas Constitution, 8–15
Texas/Republic of Texas
  acquisition attempts regarding, 33–34
  American interest in, 31
  Annexation Convention of, 86
  annexation support in, 104
  Britain's viewpoint regarding, 54–55
  in Coahuila y Tejas, 8, 10, 13, 32
  constitution of, 6–15
  Declaration of Independence of, 111n8
  defense of, 86
  diplomatic recognition of, 42
  elections in, 39, 77–79
  filibuster campaigns for, 32
  foreign policy and, 45, 46
  immigration to, 32–33, 41
  incursions into, 49, 50, 86–87, 94
  leadership characteristics in, 95
  mediation regarding, 56
  Mexico's proposal regarding, 57
  military challenges of, 50–51
  in Provincias Internas, 32
  secession and, 90
  sectional politics regarding, 2, 105
  significance of, 1, 2
  as slave state, 1, 2, 40–41, 57, 59–60, 124n36
  statehood of, 86
  territorial claims regarding, 46
Tocqueville, Alexis De, 7
Toombs, Robert, 81–82
Treaty of Velasco, 39, 41
Tulis, Jeffrey, 103
Twelfth Amendment, 12
Twenty-Fifth Amendment, 28
Tyler, John
  as accidental president, 26–30, 102
  admissions clause interpretation by, 101
  Andrew Jackson and, 22–24, 25
  after annexation, 88–92
  annexation signing by, 83–84
  annexation viewpoint of, 2–3, 51, 54, 58–63, 67, 96, 97–98, 103
  appointments by, 29–30, 59, 63–64
  assessing, 106–107
  background of, 16
  cabinet of, 99
  Calhoun's letter and, 67
  challenges of, 48
  Congress and, 30, 102–103
  as Congressman, 17–19
  constitutional interpretation by, 100–102
  criticism of, 71, 81
  death of, 91
  education of, 16–17
  Force Bill viewpoint of, 23
  as governor of Virginia, 20
  Hawaii and, 101
  Henry Clay and, 26, 28, 29
  illness of, 18
  influence of, 3
  inspirations of, 16–17
  John Quincy Adams and, 22
  military actions of, 68
  Missouri Compromise viewpoint of, 18–19
  Missouri speech of, 18, 19
  national prominence rise of, 25–26
  presidential power and, 4
  prioritization by, 53–54
  removal power provision and, 99–100
  as running mate, 25–26
  Sam Houston and, 88–89
  secession crisis and, 90–91
  secret service fund use by, 100, 132n12
  sectional politics and, 105
  as Senator, 20–25
  slavery viewpoint of, 64
  term limit of, 97–98
  territorial expansion viewpoint of, 19, 20–21, 30
  third-party coalition of, 75
  vetoes of, 29
  vision of, 20–21
  at Washington Peace Conference, 90–91
  Whig Party and, 24–25, 27–28, 29, 48, 102

Tyler, John (*continued*)
    withdrawal of, 76–77
Tyler, John, Sr., 16
Tyler, Lyon, 17
Tyler Doctrine, 101, 106

Upshur, Abel, 52–53, 59, 60, 61–62, 63
U. S. S. Princeton, 63

Van Buren, Martin
    Andrew Jackson and, 72–73
    annexation of Texas viewpoint of, 42–43, 70, 71–72, 105
    campaign of, 25, 41
    Democratic Party and, 43
    election of, 26
    nomination of, 73
    two-party system and, 21
Van Zandt, Isaac, 54, 58, 59, 61, 63, 65
Vasquez, Rafael, 49
vice president, constitutional requirements of, 10
Virginia
    as Confederate States capital, 91
    as "Mother of Presidents," 3

Walker, Robert J., 62, 83
Washington, George, 10, 93
Washington Peace Conference, 90–91
Webster, Daniel, 24, 25, 28, 29, 35, 52, 54, 59, 99, 105
Webster-Ashburton Treaty, 53, 100, 132n12
Whig Party
    agenda of, 28–29
    annexation viewpoint of, 81
    candidates of, 25–26
    Henry Clay's nomination by, 70–71, 73, 74–75
    John Tyler and, 24–25, 27–28, 29, 48, 102
    origin of, 24
    removal power viewpoint of, 99
Whiskey Rebellion, 10
White, Hugh Lawson, 25
Wise, Henry, 51–52, 64
Woll, Adrian, 50

Zacatecas, Mexico, 38
Zavala, Lorenzo de, 7

www.ingramcontent.com/pod-product-compliance
Lightning Source LLC
Chambersburg PA
CBHW030656230426

43665CB00011B/1121